# NO LONGER A TARE
## Converting the Christian Believer Workbook

Cassandra L. Valentine

Copyright © 2021 by **Cassandra L. Valentine**

All rights reserved. No part of this publication may be reproduced, distributed or transmitted in any form or by any means, including photocopying, recording, or other electronic or mechanical methods, without the prior written permission of the publisher, except in the case of brief quotations embodied in critical reviews and certain other noncommercial uses permitted by copyright law. For permission requests, write to the publisher, addressed "Attention: Permissions Coordinator," at the address below.

**Cassandra L. Valentine/Rejoice Essential Publishing**

PO BOX 512

Effingham, SC 29541

www.republishing.org

Unless otherwise indicated, scripture is taken from the King James Version.'

The Holy Bible, Berean Study Bible, BSB Copyright ©2016, 2020 by Bible Hub Used by Permission. All Rights Reserved Worldwide.

Scripture quotations marked (NIV) are taken from the Holy Bible, New International Version®, NIV®. Copyright © 1973, 1978, 1984, 2011 by Biblica, Inc.™ Used by permission of Zondervan. All rights reserved worldwide. www.zondervan.com The "NIV" and "New International Version" are trademarks registered in the United States Patent and Trademark Office by Biblica, Inc.™

The Holy Bible, English Standard Version® (ESV®) Copyright © 2001 by Crossway, a publishing ministry of Good News Publishers. All rights reserved. ESV Text Edition: 2016

Scripture taken from the New King James Version®. Copyright © 1982 by Thomas Nelson. Used by permission. All rights reserved.

Scripture quotations marked MSG are taken from THE MESSAGE, copyright © 1993, 2002, 2018 by Eugene H. Peterson. Used by permission of NavPress, represented by Tyndale House Publishers. All rights reserved.

Scripture quotations marked (NLT) are taken from the Holy Bible, New Living Translation, copyright ©1996, 2004, 2015 by Tyndale House Foundation. Used by permission of Tyndale House Publishers, Carol Stream, Illinois 60188. All rights reserved.

**No Longer A Tare/ Cassandra L. Valentine**

ISBN-13: 978-1-952312-90-8

# DEDICATION

To my Lord and King, Jesus Christ, thank you for the privilege and honor to serve you.

To my husband Paul Valentine Sr., thank you for giving up time with me so that I could complete this work. Your love, support, and encouragement will forever be cherished.

# TABLE OF CONTENTS

**MODULE 1:** **LIFE IN CHRIST**..................................................ix
    ETERNAL SALVATION..........................................1
    WHY MUST WE BE SAVED...................................1
    THE NEW CREATION............................................3
    THE PROCESS OF SALVATION............................5
    SALVATION AND GRACE....................................15
    REPENTANCE: SALVATION'S
    PRIMARY PREREQUISITE................................18
    THE OUTCOME...................................................22

**MODULE 2:** **YOUR RELATIONSHIP WITH GOD**................24
    WHO IS GOD?.......................................................25
    A CONSISTENT DEVOTIONAL LIFE.................33
    DAILY PRAYER...................................................34
    BEING FILLED WITH THE HOLY SPIRIT.........38
    PRAYING DAILY IN THE HOLY SPIRIT............39
    STUDYING THE WORD......................................40

**MODULE 3:** **CULTIVATING GODLINESS**...........................45
    THE FRUIT OF THE SPIRIT..............................47
    THE GIFTS OF THE SPIRIT..............................59

**MODULE 4:** **BIBLICAL CHURCH MEMBERSHIP**..............70
    A CALL TO SERVE..............................................72
    COMMITMENT.....................................................75
    GROWING IN UNITY..........................................76
    UNDERSTANDING HONOR...............................87

| | |
|---|---|
| HONORING OTHERS | 88 |
| GIVING | 89 |
| ABOUT THE AUTHOR | 98 |

# MODULE 1

LIFE IN CHRIST

# ETERNAL SALVATION

When asked to explain salvation, the average Christian will say that it is centered on God saving us from eternal punishment in hell by forgiveness of sin. Salvation is a more complex process than is often understood. When we reduce salvation to just escaping the punishment of hell, we limit God's plan for our lives. Salvation is an invitation to eternal citizenship in the Kingdom of God, and it comes with benefits <u>and</u> responsibilities.

### WHY MUST WE BE SAVED

Before receiving salvation, Scripture tells us that we are spiritually dead.

John 5:24 [NKJV]- "Most assuredly, I say to you, he who hears My word and believes in Him who sent Me has everlasting life, and shall not come into judgment, but has passed from <u>death into life</u>."

Ephesians 2:1-3 [NKJV] also describes our state before salvation:

"And you He made alive, who were <u>dead in trespasses and sins</u>, in which you once walked according to the course of this world, according to the prince of the power of the air, the spirit who now works in the sons of disobedience, among whom also we all once conducted ourselves in the lusts of our flesh, fulfilling the desires of the flesh and of the mind, and were by nature children of wrath, just as the others."

Several points are made in these two passages of Scripture about a person's condition, state, and status before receiving salvation:

1) They are spiritually dead.
2) Judgment is their inheritance, not everlasting life.
3) They are guilty of trespasses and sins.
4) They have the spirit of Satan working in them.
5) They fulfill the desires of the flesh and mind.
6) They are the children of wrath.

Re-read both John 5:24 and Ephesians 2:1-3 and identify all six points listed above.

Acts 26:18 [NKJV]also gives insight into our condition before salvation:

"...to open their eyes, in order to turn them from darkness to light, and from the power of Satan to God, that they may receive forgiveness of sins and an inheritance among those who are sanctified by faith in Me."

In addition to the six points listed above, Acts 26:18 identifies four additional facts about the unsaved:

1) They are spiritually blind.
2) They are citizens of the Kingdom of darkness.
3) They are under Satan's power.
4) They have no forgiveness of sins.

The chart below summarizes what we have discovered so far.

| NOT SAVED | SAVED |
| --- | --- |
| Spiritually dead | Made alive by Jesus |
| Spiritually blind | Eyes are open |
| Will receive God's judgment | Saved from judgment |
| Guilty of trespasses and sin | Forgiven |
| Have the spirit of Satan working in them | Have the Spirit of Christ working in them |
| Fulfills the desires of their flesh and mind | No longer fulfills the desires of their flesh and mind |
| Children of wrath | Children of God |
| Citizens of Satan's Kingdom | Citizens of God's Kingdom |
| Under Satan's power | No longer under Satan's power |

Now, we have established the spiritual condition of people before salvation. In the following section, we will review what happens upon receiving salvation.

## THE NEW CREATION

[2 Corinthians 5:17 NKJV] "Therefore, if anyone is in Christ, he is a new creation; old things have passed away; behold, all things have become new."

According to 2 Corinthians 5:17, when a person becomes saved or "receives" salvation, they become a new creation. The Merriam-Webster dictionary defines the word new as "having been seen, used, or known for a short time.'"

---

1. Definition of NEW." Merriam-Webster.com, 2018, www.merriam-webster.com/dictionary/new.

For some, this will be hard to believe: when God says something, He means what He says. God's Word tells us that we become "a new creation," and we are just that – new. In John 5:24, Jesus declares that a person goes from death to life. God swaps out the dead spirit and replaces it with a brand-new spirit, filled with His light. Isn't that great news!

Ezekiel 36:26-27 NKJV also talks about the new spirit and new heart we receive when saved:

> "I will give you a new heart and put a new spirit within you; I will take the heart of stone out of your flesh and give you a heart of flesh. I will put My Spirit within you and cause you to walk in My statutes, and you will keep My judgments and do them."

God does miraculous work in us when we receive salvation!

[2 Corinthians 5:17 NKJV] "Therefore, if anyone is in Christ, he is a new creation; <u>old things have passed away; behold, all things have become new.</u>"

When God has replaced these past things, the newly saved person won't behave the same way. They will see things differently upon salvation. Activities and behaviors that were once appealing will become appalling. Their eyes will be opened (Acts 26:18).

2 Corinthians 5:17 tells us that we become *different* immediately upon receiving salvation. Merriam Webster defines *"different"* as be-

ing "partly or totally *unlike* in nature, form, or quality.[2]"  The very essence of our nature changes.

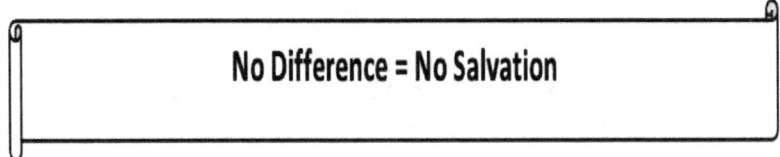
No Difference = No Salvation

We cannot assume that everyone who prays the prayer of salvation is saved. But, if we are saved, there will be evidence of it. Thus, not only does genuine salvation make us different people, but it also makes us different from the rest of the world and the rest of all creation.

If someone believes they are saved but have not changed in any way, they have not received or experienced true salvation. However, this does not mean their attire or mannerisms will be perfect or even ideal after receiving salvation . The miraculous change that occurs with salvation happens on the inside first and then will eventually show outwardly.  For example, a prostitute who receives genuine salvation may present their prior lifestyle until thoroughly discipled. Therefore, it is critical to the success and development of the new convert to be immersed in teaching and discipleship immediately following salvation.

## THE PROCESS OF SALVATION

Salvation is a process, and it is conditional. Yes, it is a gift from God, but there are strings attached. Listed below are some of the conditions of authentic salvation:

---

2. "Definition of DIFFERENT." Www.merriam-Webster.com, www.merriam-webster.com/dictionary/different.

1. **We must repent** – [Acts 3:19 NKJV] *"Repent therefore and be converted, that your sins may be blotted out, so that times of refreshing may come from the presence of the Lord."*

    - The subject of repentance is covered in more detail later in this study. But we must understand this: repentance and conversion go hand in hand; transformation cannot occur without repentance.

2. **We must believe and be saved** – [Mark 16:16 NKJV] *"He who believes and is baptized will be saved; but he who does not believe will be condemned."* [Also see 1 Cor 15:1-2]

    - Jesus is speaking directly to <u>belief</u> in Him and His Word. This belief must be in your heart, not simply a confession out of your mouth. It is not enough to believe what another person told you about Jesus and His Word – you must personally believe that Jesus can save your soul [Hebrews 10:39].

3. **We must live according to the Spirit** – [Romans 8:12-14 NKJV] *"Therefore, brethren, we are debtors—not to the flesh, to live according to the flesh. For if you live according to the flesh you will die; but if by the Spirit you put to death the deeds of the body, you will live. For as many as are led by the Spirit of God, these are sons of God."*

    - Galatians chapter 5, which we will explore in more detail later in this study, describes the difference between living and walking according to the Spirit of God versus being led by the flesh (our dark human nature). Living according to the Spirit means to put to death (or stop indulging in) the deeds of the flesh. As you will learn later in this study, it is impossible to live according to the Spirit if you are led by the flesh – as they are in direct opposition to one another.

4. **We must bring forth fruit** – [John 15:5-8 NKJV] *"I am the vine; you are the branches. He who abides in Me, and I in him, bears much fruit; for without Me you can do nothing. If anyone does not abide in Me, he is cast out as a branch and is withered; and they gather them and throw them into the fire, and they are burned. If you abide in Me, and My words abide in you, you will ask what you desire, and it shall be done for you. By this My Father is glorified, that you bear much fruit; so you will be My disciples."*

   - Jesus makes it clear that when we are abiding in Him, there <u>will be</u> much fruit. If there is no fruit, then we are not abiding in Him. The fruit He is speaking of is the fruit of the Spirit, which we cover later in this study. This fruit is the evidence that He is abiding in us. Keep in mind that this is not "on-again, off-again" fruit, but consistent and persistent fruit. An indication that His words abide in you is that you obey and do His Word no matter what. James 1:22 declares that we are deceiving ourselves if we are only hearers but not doers of the Word.

5. **Holiness is required** – [1 Peter 1:13-16 NKJV] *"Therefore gird up the loins of your mind, be sober, and rest your hope fully upon the grace that is to be brought to you at the revelation of Jesus Christ; as obedient children, not conforming yourselves to the former lusts, as in your ignorance; but as He who called you is holy, you also be holy in all your conduct, because it is written, "Be holy, for I am holy."'*

- Notice that the command is to be holy, not told to try our best to be holy. This passage of Scripture says a lot about holiness, but if we "hone in" on the part that says, "be holy in all your conduct," it is the clear and indisputable understanding that the author of Hebrews is referring to the way we behave. This includes, but is certainly not limited to:
    1) the way we treat people,
    2) consistently demonstrate self-control,
    3) not participating in or being associated with sin,
    4) exhibiting the fruit of the Spirit, and
    5) even how we dress.

Whether you want to believe it or not, our dress is a direct link to our behavior. If we dress seductively, we are behaving like a seductress. If we dress like a thug, we are acting like a thug. To be clear, we are not to assume that because someone dresses modestly, they are holy, but we can infer from our dress if we act unholy. Hebrews 12:14 makes it clear that without holiness, we will not see the Lord. Holiness is not a request or suggestion but a requirement of salvation. We must practice holiness.

6. **We must endure until the end** – [Matthew 24:13 NKJV] *"But he who endures to the end shall be saved."*

- Jesus makes it clear in this verse that we will only be saved if we endure to the end of our life or the end of this world. Meaning, we must continue in the way of Christ until the end of our human life to receive His reward. In Matthew 24, the Disciples were asking Jesus about when the end of the world would be: they wanted to know how to recognize the signs. In your own time, read verses 3-14 to get the full context of what He was teaching them. One thing He shared was that lawlessness would abound, and the love of many would grow cold. Jesus was explaining to them how bad things would get in the world and for the believer. Regardless of what is to come, to be saved (to inherit the Kingdom), we must endure all tribulation. Giving up is not an option if we are to be saved. We can live for Christ for 20 years, obeying His Word and doing great work for Him, but if we faint or give up, before the end of our life, none of what we did or how we lived will count.

7. **Obedience** – [John 14:23 NKJV] - *Jesus answered and said to him, "If anyone loves Me, he will keep My word; and My Father will love him, and We will come to him and make Our home with him. He who does not love Me does not keep My words; and the word which you hear is not Mine but the Father's who sent Me."*

- Jesus could not have been clearer – if we don't obey His Word, we don't love Him. And if we do not love Him, God the Father will not love us and will not live in us. Read this verse again. Understand that this is not my opinion but the Word of the Lord. There is no reason that we can present before God that will justify our disobedience. His Word tells us repeatedly not to sin. If we sin, we are directly disobeying God and disqualified from entering the Kingdom. Obedience is paramount – it is not optional, nor is it circumstantial.

8. **No more willful sin** – [Hebrews 10:26-31 NKJV] *"For if we sin willfully after we have received the knowledge of the truth, there no longer remains a sacrifice for sins, but a certain fear-*

*ful expectation of judgment, and fiery indignation which will devour the adversaries. Anyone who has rejected Moses' law dies without mercy on the testimony of two or three witnesses. Of how much worse punishment, do you suppose, will he be thought worthy who has trampled the Son of God underfoot, counted the blood of the covenant by which he was sanctified a common thing, and insulted the Spirit of grace? For we know Him who said, "Vengeance is Mine, I will repay," says the Lord. And again, "The Lord will judge His people." It is a fearful thing to fall into the hands of the living God."*

- To continue in sin means that Jesus' sacrifice on the cross no longer applies to you. Of course, not unless you repent (covered in the following sections). To sum it up nicely, when we continue to sin after receiving salvation and being taught, the Scripture says

1. we should have a fearful expectation of judgment,
2. we have done the equivalent of trampling Jesus underfoot by treating His sacrifice as a common thing, and
3. we have insulted the Spirit of grace.

ASSIGNMENT

**Complete the following exercise**
Read **1 John 3:4-9** and answer the questions that follow.
1. What is sin according to verse 4?

_____

_____

2. What does verse 6 say about the person who abides in God?

_____

_____

_____

3. What does verse 8 say about the person who sins?

_____

_____

_____

4. What does verse 9 say about the one who has been born of God?

_____

_____

_____

**The greatest threat to our salvation is sin. Answer the additional questions below about sin:**

1. Read Hebrews 10:26-27 again. What does it say we can expect because of willful sin?

_____

_____

_____

2. What do you understand willful sin to be?

_____

_____

_____

3. Read Isaiah 59:2. What does it say happens because of sin?

_____

_____

_____

4. What does Romans 6:23 say is the consequence of sin?

_____

_____

_____

5. What does John 8:34 say about those that sin?

_____

_____

_____

Hopefully, you can now see what an active part you play in your salvation. But, unfortunately, saying a prayer does not guarantee salvation. Believing that it does results in development of a false sense of security regarding salvation. Below you will find a list of false assurances people may have regarding salvation:

▶ **Professing salvation.** [Matthew 7:21-23 NKJV] *Not everyone who says to Me, 'Lord, Lord,' shall enter the Kingdom of heaven, but he who does the will of My Father in heaven. Many will say to Me, in that day, 'Lord, Lord, have we not prophesied in Your name, cast out demons in Your name, and done many wonders in Your name?' And then I will declare to them, 'I <u>never</u> knew you; depart from Me, you who practice lawlessness!'*

Jesus did not say you will know them because they prayed a prayer or made a profession. He said you would know them by their fruit (Matthew 7:20). Every saved person will profess their faith in Jesus. But not every person that professes faith in Jesus is a believer. Also, notice that Jesus did not deny or dispute that these people had prophesied, cast out demons, or performed signs and wonders. Why is this important? Unfortunately, many believe that by operating in spiritual gifts, God must be pleased. However, this is a dangerous thing to assume. Anyone could use their spiritual gifts and still miss eternal salvation.

▶ **Belief in God.** [John 14:1 KJV] *"Let not your heart be troubled; you believe in God, believe also in Me."*

The entire demonic realm believes in God. The religious leaders Jesus called vipers and hypocrites believed in God. But Jesus told them that they were of their father, the devil, and did not belong to God (See John 8:42-47). Our ability to hear, believe, and receive God's Word, makes us His – not just a <u>belief</u> in Him.

▶ **Church Membership.** [2 Corinthians 13:5 NKJV] *"Examine yourselves as to whether you are in the faith. Test yourselves. Do* *you not know yourselves, that Jesus Christ is in you? —unless indeed you are disqualified."*

Apostle Paul, while addressing the Corinthian church, called upon these believers to examine themselves regularly. It is important to note that faithfully attending a church does not make one saved.

▶ **Water Baptism.** [Mark 16:16 NKJV] *"He who believes and is baptized will be saved; but he who does not believe will be condemned."*

Everyone who professes salvation should follow through with baptism. But not everyone who is baptized is saved. A person gets baptized because they are saved – not to <u>become</u> saved.

▶ **Once saved, always saved.** [James 5:19-20 NKJV] *"Brethren, if anyone among you wanders from the truth, and someone turns him back, let him know that he who turns a sinner from the error of his way will save a soul from death and cover a multitude of sins.*

Scripture does not support the doctrine of "once saved always saved." James tells us that we can wander from the truth and receive death as a reward. We see clearly from Hebrews 10:26-39 that sin revokes our salvation status.

There is no sin in God's Kingdom. The sin that was there was removed when Lucifer and a third of the angels were kicked out of Heaven (see Isaiah 14:12-14 and Ezekiel 28:14-16). God has a responsibility to the citizens in His Kingdom, to not allow sin to come back there. Therefore, to practice sin "because we can't can't help it" is not an excuse and will prevent us from inheriting the Kingdom and receiving eternal security.

God requires for us to be pure and clean, as noted in Ephesians 5:25-27 [NKJV]: —

> " Husbands, love your wives, just as Christ also loved the church and gave Himself for her, that He might sanctify and cleanse her with the washing of water by the word, that He might present her to Himself a glorious church, not having spot or wrinkle or any such thing, but that she should be holy and without blemish."

The reference to blemishes in the above passage is not about physical appearance but about the church being pure before the Lord. To be "without blemish" is to be without a mark or problem. The same standard God had in the Old Testament about the animals used in sacrificial offerings. The animals could not have any "blemish." God requires we come before Him with clean hands and a pure heart [Psalm 24:3-4 NKJV]: —

> "Who may ascend into the hill of the Lord? Or who may stand in His holy place? He who has clean hands and a pure heart, who has not lifted up his soul to an idol, nor sworn deceitfully."

## SALVATION AND GRACE

While addressing the Corinthian church, Apostle Paul says this in 2 Corinthians 6:1-2 *"We then, as workers together with Him also plead with you not to receive the grace of God in vain. For He says: "In an acceptable time I have heard you, and in the day of salvation I have helped you."* The day when we receive salvation, we also receive His help – that help is His grace. The Merriam-Webster Dictionary defines grace as the "…unmerited divine assistance given to humans for their regeneration or sanctification.[3]"

---

3. "Definition of GRACE." Www.merriam-Webster.com, www.merriam-webster.com/dictionary/grace.

An exaggerated doctrine of grace taught in some churches states that the believer is no longer required to repent of any past, present, or future sin upon salvation. Yet, Scripture opposes this belief, as seen in the passages below. Read each, and discuss as a group what you learn from these verses:

▶ 2 Peter 2:20-21 [NKJV]: *"For if, after they have escaped the pollutions of the world through the knowledge of the Lord and Savior Jesus Christ, they are again entangled in them and overcome, the latter end is worse for them than the beginning. For it would have been better for them not to have known the way of righteousness, than having known it, to turn from the holy commandment delivered to them."*

▶ Ezekiel 33:12-13 [NKJV]: *"...The righteousness of the righteous man shall not deliver him in the day of his transgression; as for the wickedness of the wicked, he shall not fall because of it in the day that he turns from his wickedness; nor shall the righteous be able to live because of his righteousness in the day that he sins. When I say to the righteous that he shall surely live, but he trusts in his own righteousness and commits iniquity, none of his righteous works shall be remembered; but because of the iniquity that he has committed, he shall die."*

▶ Galatians 6:7-8 [NKJV]: *"Do not be deceived, God is not mocked; for whatever a man sows, that he will also reap. For he who sows to his flesh reap corruption, but he who sows to the Spirit will of the Spirit reap everlasting life."*

▶ Romans 6:15 [NKJV]: *"What then? Shall we sin because we are not under law but under grace? Certainly not! Do you not know that to whom you present yourselves slaves to obey, you are that one's slaves whom you obey, whether of sin leading to death, or of obedience leading to righteousness?"*

You may have heard that we are no longer under the law. Yes, believers are under grace and not the law, but what does that mean?

**A look at Jeremiah 31:31-34 [NKJV]:**

*"Behold, the days are coming, says the Lord, when I will make a new covenant with the house of Israel and with the house of Judah – not according to the covenant that I made with their fathers in the day that I took them by the hand to lead them out of the land of Egypt, My covenant which they broke, though I was a husband to them, says the Lord. But this is the covenant that I will make with the house of Israel after those days, says the Lord: I will put My <u>law</u> in their minds, and write it on their hearts; and I will be their God, and they shall be my people."*

If the law is no longer relevant (in the new covenant), what will God put in the minds of His people and write on their hearts?

**Psalm 19:7 The law of the Lord is perfect, converting the soul.**

The "law" says we shouldn't do this and don't do that. It is considered bondage to the lawless. Regardless of what people may feel or believe about the law, Psalm 19 tells us that God's law plays a vital role in our conversion. Upon receiving salvation, we not only receive a new heart (with God's law already written on it), but we receive His grace that empowers us not to do or want to do the things that violate His law.

The law is how we know what sin is. Romans 3:20b NKJV says, *"for by the law is the knowledge of sin."* The law exposes sin's presence.

**Romans 7:7-12** NKJV – *"What shall we say then? Is the law sin? Certainly not! On the contrary, I would not have known sin except through the law. For I would not have known covetousness unless the law had said, "You shall not covet."*

What we must understand is that the entire Word of God (our King) is the law! To say we are no longer under the law would mean that we could throw the Ten Commandments in the trash, and are now free to kill, still, covet, have other gods, etc. To declare that God's law no longer binds us to the law means there are no standards, rules, stipulations, guidelines, etc., for us to follow.

## REPENTANCE – SALVATION'S IMMEDIATE PRE-REQUISITE

In the previous section, repentance is the first condition in the process of salvation. There are two scenarios in which repentance is necessary: 1) for initial salvation 2) and sin committed after salvation. To have a clear understanding of what repentance is, review the definition below:

a) Easton's Bible Dictionary defines "repentance" (metanoeo, metanoevw), as "meaning to change one's mind and purpose, as the result of after knowledge. This verb, a (3) cognate noun "metanoia", is used in describing true repentance, a change of mind and purpose and life, to which remission of sin is promised.[4]

---

[4] "Repentance - Biblical Meaning of Repentance in Eastons Bible Dictionary (Bible History Online)." Www.bible-History.com, www.bible-history.com/eastons/r/repentance/. Accessed 25 June 2021

This definition teaches that repentance involves turning from sin, and not turning back as a requirement for salvation. True repentance means to stop a vile, wicked, sinful behavior and not do it again. Christians must understand that repentance is not an apology. To continue a behavior repeatedly, with prayers of "I'm sorry" in-between, does not mean that God has forgiven us of those sins. In 2 Corinthians 7:9-10 [NKJV], the Apostle wrote, *"Now I rejoice, not that you were made sorry, but that your sorrow led to repentance. For you were made sorry in a godly manner, that you might suffer loss from us in nothing. For godly sorrow produces repentance leading to salvation, not to be regretted; but the sorrow of the world produces death (emphasis added).*" Paul is telling us here that truly sorrowful or repentant people won't do it again. This sadness over our disobedience before God is what produces repentance; thus, leading to salvation.

The devil cannot fully control Christians. When a believer sins, they make a fully conscious and willing decision to commit that sin. So to say "the devil made me do it" is a lie; he can only suggest or tempt you to sin – but he cannot physically make you do it.

 **ASSIGNMENT**

**Review each of the following Scriptures about repentance and answer the questions listed for each one.**

1.  Acts 3:19 [NKJV] declares, *"Repent therefore and be converted, that your sins may be blotted out, so that times of refreshing may come from the presence of the Lord."*

**Look up the definition of "converted" and explain what it means.**

_____

_____

_____

2. 2 Timothy 2:24-26 [NKJV] states, *"And a servant of the Lord must not quarrel but be gentle to all, able to teach, patient, in humility correcting those who are in opposition, if God perhaps will grant them repentance, so that they may know the truth."*

**Based on this Scripture, is repentance guaranteed? Why or why not?**

_____

_____

_____

3. Read Romans 1:28-32 in the King James Version of the Bible.

**Look up the definition of the word "reprobate," and write the definition below:**

_____

_____

_____

**Once God has turned someone over to a reprobate mind, will they ever be able to repent again? Will they feel the need? Why or why not?**

_____

_____

From this study on repentance, we learn the following:
1. God desires for us all to repent.
2. Repentance means to turn not just to apologize.
3. God must grant repentance; it is a gift and is therefore not guaranteed.
4. If we fail to repent and continue in sin, God, at any time, can turn us over to a mind that does not see or feel the need to repent.

Consider all that you have learned in this study so far and take some time to do a self-examination. Are you saved? Have you truly repented of your sins? Are you struggling with the conditions listed in "The Process of Salvation" described on page 4 in this workbook?

Doctrines of devils include teaching believers that God understands and sympathizes with our sin plight. You might have been comforted by teaching that suggests that as long as you try not to sin, you would still inherit the Kingdom and everlasting life with Christ if you were to die today. Many teachings on grace suggest and outright declare that you only have to do your best because of God's grace, and all will be well between you and God. After this study, do you still believe that?

One commonly misquoted and misapplied Scripture is Romans 8:1 [NKJV], which says, *"There is therefore now no condemnation to those that are in Christ Jesus, <u>who do not walk according to the flesh, but according to the Spirit.</u>"* When quoting and standing on this Scripture, most people will stop at "Jesus" and omit the last part of the passage. There are two reasons for this: 1) people purposely quote just the first part because it seemingly backs their position, or 2) the version of the Bible they are using has erased the rest of the verse after "Jesus," and people do not know the rest of the verse exists. Whatever the reason, the truth is that you haven't received Christ if sin is present in your life. Sin brings only death and condemnation.

## THE OUTCOME

We learn from Romans 2:6-11 [NJKV] that God rewards us according to our deeds (behaviors; actions),

> "Who will render to each one according to his deeds": eternal life to those who by patient continuance in doing good seek for glory, honor, and immortality; but to those who are self-seeking and do not obey the truth, but obey unrighteousness—indignation and wrath, tribulation and anguish, on every soul of man who does evil, of the Jew first and also of the Greek; but glory, honor, and peace to everyone who works what is good, to the Jew first and also to the Greek. For there is no partiality with God."

It is not enough to start well; we must continue to do well. In the above passage, notice that "wrath, tribulation and anguish" will be the outcome for every soul who does evil. It did not say "on every soul who does evil, except the ones who prayed the prayer of salvation." Hell is the destination for every person that does evil.

What is evil? Evil is wicked behavior; works of the flesh. Galatians 5:19-21 [NKJV] spells it out for us —

> "Now the works of the flesh are evident, which are: adultery, fornication, uncleanness, lewdness, idolatry, sorcery, hatred, contentions, jealousies, outbursts of wrath, selfish ambitions, dissensions, heresies, envy, murders, drunkenness, revelries, and the like; of which I tell you beforehand, just as I told you in time past, that those who practice such things will not inherit the Kingdom of God."

Notice after revelries, it says "and the like" – meaning, anything that is like any of those works listed. People will often say things like, "the Bible doesn't specifically say you can't do…". The phrase "and the like" invalidates that argument.

 **ASSIGNMENT**

**Spend some time reviewing each of the works of the flesh listed above. Research each term to get a clear meaning of each.**

As previously discussed in this module, salvation is work – it is a process. The work of salvation is not to be confused with "doing works" like feeding the hungry, doing nice things for people, being a good person, serving in the church, obeying the laws of the land, etc. Philippians 2:12 tells us to "…work out your own salvation with fear and trembling." If receiving salvation was only saying a prayer, then what is there for us to work out? And why do we have to do it with fear and trembling?

Simply put, that "work" refers to our complete and total obedience to God and His Word. Whatever Scripture says not to do,– don't do. Whatever Scripture says to do – you do. The only "work" God expects us to do for salvation is to OBEY HIM AND HIS WORD!

# MODULE 2

YOUR RELATIONSHIP WITH GOD

# YOUR RELATIONSHIP WITH GOD

To build any healthy relationship, you must know the person with whom you are building a relationship. There is no way for you to know a person without spending quality time with them. The same goes for building your relationship with God. To begin building your relationship with God, you first must know <u>who</u> God is.

## WHO IS GOD?

**God is Creator! Every being, human or otherwise, was given life by Creator God.**

[Acts 17:24-25 NKJV] "God, who <u>made the world and everything in it,</u> since He is <u>Lord of heaven and earth</u>, does not dwell in temples made with hands. Nor is He worshipped with men's hands, as though He needed anything, since <u>He gives to all life, breath, and all things</u>." Thus, before the world existed, God existed.

[1 Timothy 6:15 NKJV] "…He who is the blessed and only <u>Potentate</u>, the <u>King of kings</u> and <u>Lord of lords</u>"

The word potentate means "sovereign, monarch, or ruler.[5]" God is the King over every king and the Lord over every lord. There is no one above Him nor equal to Him, and that includes Satan and his kingdom.

**God is <u>One</u> God, but Three Persons:**

<u>God, the Father</u>

[Psalm 89:26 NKJV] *"He shall cry to Me, 'You are my Father, My God, and the rock of my salvation."*

<u>God, the Son (Jesus Christ)</u>

[Isaiah 9:6 NKJV] *For unto us a Child is born, unto us a Son is given; and the government will be upon His shoulder. And His name will be called Wonderful, Counselor, Mighty God, Everlasting Father, Prince of Peace.*

<u>God, the Holy Spirit</u>

[Acts 5:3-4 NKJV] *But Peter said, "Ananias, why has Satan filled your heart to lie to the Holy Spirit and keep back part of the price of the land for yourself? While it remained, was it not your own? And after it was sold, was it not in your own control? Why have you conceived this thing in your heart? You have not lied to men but to God."*

Throughout Scripture, the pronouns He, Him, Me, My, and I are all used to refer to God. We use pronouns when referring to a person. And yes, God is a person! As persons, we have a soul. God also has a

---

5 "Definition of Potentate | Dictionary.com." Www.dictionary.com, www.dictionary.com/browse/potentate. Accessed 25 June 2021.

soul. In Isaiah 42:1 [NKJV], God is speaking and says, *"Behold! My servant whom I uphold, My Elect One in whom My soul delights!"*

The soul houses the mind, will, and emotions. Therefore, God thinks, has a will, and feels emotions just as we do.

 **ASSIGNMENT**

**God Is Omnipotent, Omnipresent and Omniscient**

Write the definitions of each in the space provided:

1) Omnipotent -

_____

_____

_____

2) Omnipresent -

_____

_____

_____

3) Omniscient -

_____

_____

_____

Next, look up and read the following Scriptures, and for each, write what they say about God and note if it speaks of His Omnipotence, Omnipresence, or Omniscience:

1) Psalm 147:5 -

_____

_____

_____

2) Psalm 139:7-10 -

_____

_____

_____

3) Psalm 139:1-4 -

_____

_____

_____

4) Psalm 94:11 -

_____

_____

_____

Based on your study of God's omnipotence, omnipresence and omniscience, answer the following questions:

1. Is there anything you can do or say that God does not see or hear?
2. Is there anywhere that you can go to hide from God?
3. If you sin, does God see it?

4. Does God know all your thoughts?
5. Is there anything that God cannot do?

Now that you know God as Creator, King, Lord, Savior, Father, Ruler, and Sovereign, you know He has all power. He sees everything. He knows everything, and is everywhere at the same time. What an awesome God we serve! While we understand this amazing God loves us, it is just as important to embrace His sovereignty. In the Book of Job, we find an excellent revelation about God's Sovereignty.

God, Himself, declared that Job was a perfect and upright man who feared God and did no evil (Job 1:8). Yet God permitted Satan to attack Job (Job 1:12). First, Satan stripped Job of his wealth and killed his children. Later, Satan got additional permission from God to strike him with a disease. Job had painful boils all over his body. Satan was given carte blanche to do whatever he wanted to do to Job, except kill him (Job 2:4-7). Read Job 1:1-5 to learn a little more about Job's character. To sum it up, Job was a husband and father; perfect and blameless; hated evil and did not sin; very wealthy with a multitude of possessions; and extremely generous. He was the greatest of all the people in his country.

As you read through Job, you will see how Job, grieving and in severe pain, cries out to God. He proclaims his innocence and confusion, almost demanding that God speak to him. Job cries out against these unjust afflictions that had come upon him. God does eventually speak directly to Job and reminds him of His sovereignty in Job 38. As sovereign, God did not ask Job for his opinion or approval. He does not ask for our opinion or approval either. After reading Chapter 38, write some insights that you learned about God as He addresses Job below.

_____

The average Christian fully embraces Jesus as Savior as the One who loves them and has rescued them from hell! However, they have difficulty embracing Jesus as Lord and Sovereign King. King's rule! They have laws, standards, and requirements. The word of a King is the law. Their actions and decisions, as Job learned, cannot be debated. Unlike Presidents, people do not elect Kings, nor are they voted out or impeached.

People in countries like America are proud of their independence. Before becoming Christians, they are free to make their own decisions. They are only required to obey the laws implemented in the land in which they live. If they do not break any laws or hurt anyone, they are free to do whatever pleases them – whatever is right in their own eyes. But when a person receives salvation, life as they once knew it is over. 1 Corinthians 6:19-20 [NKJV] says this:

> "Or do you not know that your body is the temple of the Holy Spirit who is in you, whom you have from God, and you are not your own? For you were bought at a price; therefore, glorify God in your body and in your spirit which are God's."

Once a person receives Jesus as Lord and Savior, God becomes their sovereign. Furthermore, Jesus tells us in Mark 12:30 [NKJV] of the first commandment: *"And you shall love the Lord your God with all your heart, with all your soul, with all your mind, and with all your strength."* God does not suggest but requires that we put Him and His will first above all other considerations.

There is no way God can be our Savior but not our Lord. As a believer, have you relinquished complete control of your life to God? Can you think of areas in your life where you have rejected Him as your Lord? Are you still doing what you want to do without consulting and obeying Him and His Word in those areas of your life?

 **ASSIGNMENT**

Read the following verses, and write what they say about the sovereignty of God:
1.  Psalm 103:19

___

___

___

2. Psalm 115:3

_____

_____

_____

3. Daniel 4:35

_____

_____

_____

The last topic we will cover in this section is God's holiness. Psalm 99:5 says, *"Exalt the Lord our God and worship at His footstool – He is holy."* The Bible reminds us about God's holiness and His holy habitation (Deuteronomy 26:15). The online version of the King James Bible Dictionary lists these definitions for "holy[6]":

A. "Properly, whole, entire or perfect, in a moral sense. Hence, pure in heart, temper, or dispositions; free from sin and sinful affections....'

B. "Hallowed; consecrated or set apart to a sacred use, or to the service or worship of God....'

C. "Perfectly just and good; as the holy law of God....'

D. "Sacred..."'

God says in Leviticus 22:32 [NKJV], *"You shall not profane My holy name, but I will be hallowed among the children of Israel..."*.

---

6 "King James Bible Dictionary - Reference List - Holy." King James Bible Dictionary, www.kingjamesbibledictionary.com/Dictionary/holy. Accessed 25 June 2021

God had just finished telling the children of Israel to obey His commandments. By not obeying His commandments, they would be profaning His name. The word 'profane' means to "wound or dissolve."[7] We can conclude from this that God holds His holiness and His Name in high regard. God is saying, "Don't make Me look bad because I am holy." When you think about it, we are the same way. We are protective of our image and will likely become angry if someone slandered us.

We are always to speak well of God – He is Holy! Speak well of God by only using the many titles and names found in His Word, which are used to describe who He is. To use words and phrases that are anything but holy is disrespectful and ultimately rejected by God. Take a moment to consider the words, names, and phrases you use to describe God. Are they suitable for a Holy God? Times, trends, and cultures change, but God does not (Malachi 3:6). Be careful not to use slang or follow trends when referring to God. If God has not sanctioned a term or phrase, do not use it. He is HOLY!

Not only is God holy, but He commands us, as His people, to be just as holy. See what 1 Peter 1:15-16 [NKJV] says about this:

> "but as He who called you is holy, you also be holy in all your conduct, because it is written, "Be holy, for I am holy.""

## A CONSISTENT DEVOTIONAL LIFE

Now that we have learned about Who God is, we can cultivate a relationship with Him through a consistent devotional life. In this section, we will review several methods to building a relationship

---

7 H2490 - Ḥālal - Strong's Hebrew Lexicon (Kjv)." Blue Letter Bible, www.blueletterbible.org/lexicon/h2490/kjv/wlc/0-1/. Accessed 25 June 2021.

with God. One thing to note before proceeding is there is no specific formula everyone must follow. It is only important that you dedicate time to spend with God daily.

## DAILY PRAYER

Simply put, prayer is two-way communication between God and you. When we pray to God, we are not merely telling God everything on our hearts and minds. Instead, while praying, allow God time to respond, and provide instruction when needed. How strained and dull would a relationship be if only one person did all the talking? As we learned earlier, God has a mind, will, and emotions, and He enjoys fellowship with us.

In John 10:27 [NKJV], Jesus says, *"My sheep hear My voice, and I know them, and they follow Me."* Jesus was not speaking of literal sheep but those who have accepted Him as Lord and Savior and obey and follow His Word. How you get to recognize God's voice is by spending time with Him in prayer. Spending time in prayer is the best way to become familiar with God's voice.

As we continue this subject of prayer, here are a few things to note:

- The best approach to prayer is to begin as Jesus taught His disciples to pray. He told them to begin with "Our Father" (see Matthew 6:9). Then, with the power and assistance of the Holy Spirit, you bring your prayers to God the Father in the name of the Lord Jesus Christ.

- Jesus says in John 14:13 [NKJV], *"And whatever you ask in My name, that I will do, that the Father may be glorified in the Son."* Romans 8:26 [NKJV] says, *"Likewise, the Spirit also helps in our weaknesses. For we do not know what we should pray for as we ought, but the Spirit Himself makes intercession for us with groanings which cannot be uttered."* All three Persons of God have an essential role in our prayer time.

- We can and should pray anywhere and at any time. In 1 Thessalonians 5:17, it admonishes us to pray without ceasing. Throughout the day, we are to have a conversation with God no matter the circumstance.

- Prayer should be primarily verbal, but it can be non-verbal. For example, in 1 Samuel 1:11, Hannah verbalized her prayer to God. In verses 12-13, Hannah gives us an excellent example of a non-verbal prayer. The Bible says, *"...Hannah spoke in her heart..."* while praying with no sound coming out, but her mouth is moving.

- When you pray, you must believe. So James 1:6-8 [NKJV] says, *"But let him ask in faith, with no doubting, for he who doubts is like a wave of the sea driven and tossed by the wind. For let not that man suppose that he will receive anything from the Lord; he is a double-minded man, unstable in all his ways."*

In your daily prayer time with the Lord, you may want to lay before God where you pray. Maybe you'll want to kneel by your bed? Or perhaps you want to walk and pray? Do not get programmed into one way or posture in prayer. The most important thing to remember is to pray daily.

There are several prayer methods or models that teach us how to pray. Two excellent examples are Matthew 6:9-13 and Philippians 4:6-7. In these prayers, we see all the basic but essential elements of prayer outlined below:

1. Adoration and worship of the Father; acknowledge who He is.
2. Ask for forgiveness of any sin or wrongdoing; repent.
3. Petition Him for what you need.
4. Thank Him for being who He is and for hearing your requests.
5. Supplication (intercession) for others.
6. Wrap up with adoration and worship.

Prayer should be exciting; not stressful, nor formal. Prayer should not be considered an obligation but rather as a privilege to have an audience with the Lord. (See Hebrews 4:16) As you grow in your prayer life, you will grow closer and closer to God, and He will begin to share His heart and His mind with you.

 **ASSIGNMENT**

Answer the following questions related to prayer.

1. Read Ephesians 6:18. How often are we instructed to pray?

_____

_____

_____

2. Read 1 John 5:14. How can we be certain that God hears our prayers?

_____

_____

_____

3. Read Matthew 7:7. Explain how this verse relates to prayer.

___

___

___

4. Read Mark 11:22-24. What are some key things you see about prayer in these verses?

___

___

___

5. Read Matthew 18:19-20. How can we be sure that God will answer our prayers?

___

___

___

6. Read Luke 11:9-10. What instructions are we given about prayer? If by following these instructions, what results can we expect?

___

___

___

## BEING FILLED WITH THE HOLY SPIRIT

After receiving salvation, believers need to receive the baptism (filling; indwelling) of the Holy Spirit. When someone gives their life to the Lord by way of salvation, this does not automatically happen. However, there are times when the indwelling of the Holy Spirit occurs at salvation, but this is not always the case, as you can see in Acts 19:2-6 NKJV:

> And it happened, while Apollos was at Corinth, that Paul, having passed through the upper regions, came to Ephesus. And finding some disciples he said to them, "Did you receive the Holy Spirit when you believed?" So they said to him, "We have not so much as heard whether there is a Holy Spirit." And he said to them, "Into what then were you baptized?" So they said, "Into John's baptism." Then Paul said, "John indeed baptized with a baptism of repentance, saying to the people that they should believe on Him who would come after him, that is, on Christ Jesus." When they heard this, they were baptized in the name of the Lord Jesus. And when Paul had laid hands on them, the Holy Spirit came upon them, and they spoke with tongues and prophesied.

Notice in these verses that Apostle Paul addressed believers in Jesus Christ; the Scripture describes them as disciples. They had repented of their sins and took part in the water baptism but had not received the baptism of the Holy Spirit. Jesus says in Acts 2:8, after the baptism of the Holy Spirit, we would receive power. The only way we can be true witnesses for Jesus Christ is with the indwelling of the Holy Spirit. In every Scriptural account, the baptism of the Holy Spirit was received by faith.

If you have not received the indwelling of the Holy Spirit, pray, and ask the Lord to fill you. As seen in the Scripture (see Acts 19:2), once Apostle Paul told the disciples about the Holy Spirit and laid his hands on them, they were all filled with the Holy Spirit. To be clear, the laying on of hands is a way to receive the baptism of the Holy Spirit, though it is not a requirement.

Jesus told the Apostles that the Holy Spirit is a gift, the Father's promise (see Acts 1:4). The only pre-requisite to receiving the baptism of the Holy Spirit is salvation. God wants all of his children to receive the Holy Spirit without pleading.

 **Read and reflect on Luke 11:11-13.**

## PRAYING DAILY IN THE HOLY SPIRIT

After receiving the indwelling of the Holy Spirit, we can pray in our "heavenly language." We cannot mimic this speech. It flows out of us with the direct assistance of the Holy Spirit.

Praying in our "heavenly language" is not to be confused with the gift of tongues described in 1 Corinthians 12:10, which is the ability to speak in an actual unknown language (see Acts 2:1-10).

Praying in the Holy Spirit is praying in a tongue or tongues.

Every believer filled with the Holy Spirit, living a victorious life in Christ, can pray in tongues. Here are just a few of the many benefits of praying in tongues:

1. **When we pray in tongues, we are praying directly to God.** We do not have to worry about praying amiss (swinging and missing). James 4:3 [NKJV] says, *"You ask and do not receive, because you ask amiss, that you may spend it on your pleasures. When we pray in tongues, we are praying for the will of the Father."*

2. **We build ourselves up by praying in the Spirit.** Jude 20 [KJV] says, *"But you, beloved, building up yourselves on your most holy faith, praying in the Holy Ghost."* So then, as believers, we will grow in confidence and be strengthened.
3. **When we pray in tongues, we speak mysteries.** 1 Corinthians 14:2 [NKJV] says, *"For he who speaks in a tongue does not speak to men but to God, for no one understands him; however, in the Spirit he speaks mysteries."*
4. **The Holy Spirit can help us pray.** Romans 8:26 tells us that sometimes we don't know what to pray, but the Holy Spirit knows and prays those things through us. At other times, praying for a stranger or unclear request, the solution is always to pray in the Spirit.

Pray in tongues as much as possible. Not just daily, but throughout the day!

## STUDYING THE WORD

Spending time in God's Word is extremely important because it is the only way for you to get to know Him and for you to become transformed and converted to the child of God that He wants you to become. Reasons for and benefits of spending time in the Word daily are:

- **It helps you get to know God.** The Bible is God's Word. It details His history, His Sovereignty, His experiences, instruction to His people, His ways, His mind, His commandments, His promises, His Kingdom, and the list goes on. Reading and studying the Word of God is how you learn everything you need to know about our Creator, Lord and King, and how to serve Him effectively as a believer.

- **To mature you as a believer.** Ephesians 4:23 [NKJV] says, *"...and be renewed in the spirit of your mind, and that you put on the new man which was created according to God, in true righteousness and holiness."* You cannot accomplish this outside of the Word of God. You will remain a babe in Christ; spiritually immature as indicated in Hebrews 5:13 [NKJV], "For everyone who partakes only of milk is unskilled in the word of righteousness, for he is a babe."

- **To equip you to recognize deception from false teachers.** If you do not know what the Word says, it is impossible to recognize a false doctrine. As the result of accepting and following an error, one will eventually fall away from Christ. The Apostle Paul had to address this with the church at Galatia. Paul writes in Galatians 1:6-7 [NKJV], *"I marvel that you are turning away so soon from Him who called you in the grace of Christ to a different gospel, which is not another; but there are some who trouble you and want to pervert the gospel of Christ."*

There are many other benefits to reading God's Word, such as learning to hear and recognize His voice. In John 10:27 [NJKV], Jesus says, *"My sheep hear My voice, and I know them, and they follow Me."* We learn to hear and follow the voice of the Lord by knowing His Word.

 **ASSIGNMENT**

**Spend some time reviewing each of the Scripture passages referenced below and answer the questions that follow.**

Read Psalms 1:1-3. What does meditating on God's Word reveal about a saved person? Explain.

Read Joshua 1:8. What does God tell Joshua to do? What is the expected result?

Read 2 Timothy 3:15-17. What does it say about Scripture, and what it does for a person?

When you read and study Scripture, it is critical to have the right Bible. There are many versions and translations to choose from, and some are very good. However, many of them pervert the Scripture by taking it out of context and removing Scriptures altogether. The NIV, NLT, and Message Bible are polluted with error and should be avoided. One example out of hundreds is Romans 8:1. See below how each version/translation quotes this verse:

- King James Version (KJV): *"There is therefore now no condemnation to them which are in Christ Jesus, who walk not after the flesh, but after the Spirit."*

- New King James Version (NKJV): *"There is therefore now no condemnation to those who are in Christ Jesus, who do not walk according to the flesh, but according to the Spirit."*
- New International Version (NIV): *"Therefore, there is now no condemnation for those who are in Christ Jesus."*
- New Living Translation (NLT): *"So now there is no condemnation for those who belong to Christ Jesus."*
- The Message (MSG): *"With the arrival of Jesus, the Messiah, that fateful dilemma is resolved. Those who enter into Christ's being-here-for-us-no longer, have to live under a continuous black cloud."*

So, looking at the different versions of Romans 8:1, you will notice that only KJV and NKJV include the second part of that verse. The other versions completely removed that part. Why is this important? Believers need to know that they are free from condemnation if they are NOT walking and living according to their fleshly desires. If they are walking according to the flesh, they are NOT free from condemnation. We have a role to play in our salvation, as we learned in the first module of this workbook. The Lord will not control our flesh for us; that is a decision that only we can make.

This author highly recommends using the KJV or NKJV <u>in addition</u> to other translations you choose. That way, you will notice if something was removed from the version or translation you are using. All of scripture is important, and no one has the authority to decide what verse or word is irrelevant. Nor does anyone have the authority to re-word a verse and distort its meaning. For example, Hebrews 4:12 NKJV says this about God's Word:

> "For the word of God is living and powerful, and sharper than any two-edged sword, piercing even to the division of soul and spirit, and of joints and marrow, and is a discerner of the thoughts and intents of the heart."

When people revise, modify and pervert God's Word, it can no longer meet the standards of Hebrews 4:12.

# MODULE 3

**CULTIVATING GODLINESS**

# CULTIVATING GODLINESS

As a result of Adam's sin and disobedience, all of humanity was subsequently born into sin. Romans 5:19 [NKJV] says, *"For as by one man's disobedience many were made sinners, so also by one Man's obedience many will be made righteous."* Jesus explains in John 3:5 why we must be born again, saying, *"Most assuredly, I say to you, unless one is born of water and the Spirit, he cannot enter the Kingdom of God."* When we are born again, we receive a new creation spirit, but we must learn to put off the old man and put on the new man. Ephesians 4:22-24 says:

> "...that you put off, concerning your former conduct, the old man which grows corrupt according to the deceitful lusts, and be renewed in the spirit of your mind, and that you put on the new man which was created according to God, in true righteousness and holiness."

The sinful works of the flesh are evident in the old man's obedience to the flesh. Galatians 5:19-21 has a lengthy but not exhaustive list of these works. Refer to your notes in Module One on the works of the flesh. When we put off the old man, we put to death our fleshly sin nature—making a conscious decision not to participate in sin any longer.

As discussed earlier, God gives us the gift of grace, empowering us to overcome sin and deeds of the flesh. His expectation for us is to be led by the Spirit. Galatians 5:16-18 has this to say about being led by the Spirit:

> "I say then: Walk in the Spirit, and you shall not fulfill the lust of the flesh. For the flesh lusts against the Spirit, and the Spirit against the flesh; and these are contrary to one another, so that you do not do the things that you wish. But if you are led by the Spirit, you are not under the law."

Simply put, if you are in the flesh, you are not in the Spirit – there is no gray area; it is one or the other. In the next section, you will learn how to walk in the Spirit and pinpoint where you are falling short of doing so.

## THE FRUIT OF THE SPIRIT

There are nine fruits of the Spirit according to Galatians 5:22-25 [NKJV] – *"But the fruit of the Spirit is love, joy, peace, longsuffering, kindness, goodness, faithfulness, gentleness, self-control. Against such there is no law. And those who are Christ's have crucified the flesh with its passions and desires. If we live in the Spirit, let us also walk in the Spirit."*

Notice that while there are nine fruits, they are all collectively the fruit of <u>the</u> Spirit. There is no limit to how many we produce. We should become "exceedingly" fruitful in our obedience to Christ. While a person might be "kind" or "gentle," this doesn't mean they have received Christ as Savior.

### **Love**

People often confuse love with being a warm fuzzy feeling, but love is not a feeling; it is a choice. 1 Corinthians 13:4-7 [NKJV] says: *"Love suffers long and is kind; love does not envy; love does not parade itself, is not puffed up; does not behave rudely, does not seek its own, is not provoked, thinks no evil; does not rejoice in iniquity, but rejoices in the truth; bears all things, believes all things, hopes all things, endures all things."*

When we examine this passage more closely, we can conclude that true love is demonstrated by putting others above ourselves. Love is responsibility. We also can see from these verses that love is not conditional. An excellent example of this type of love is John 3:16, which says, *"For God so loved the world that He gave His only begotten Son, that whoever believes in Him should not perish but have everlasting life."* God did not send Jesus to die for our sins because we deserved it or earned it; He chose to because He loves us.

Lastly, for those that are in Jesus Christ, love is not optional; it is a commandment. Here are the words of Jesus regarding love: *"This is my commandment, That ye love one another, as I have loved you."* [John 15:12 NKJV]

### **Joy**

One of the most extraordinary things about joy is that we are strengthened by it (see Nehemiah 8:10). When the burdens of life weigh us down, a secret weapon to get out of the slump and sadness is to get into the presence of the Lord. Psalm 16:11 [NKJV] says, *"You will show me the path of life; In Your presence is fullness of joy."*

In the most challenging life experiences, whether it is the loss of a loved one, loss of possessions, or just the overall circumstances and difficulties of life, joy is the weapon we must use to ward off depression and discontentment. In 1 Thessalonians 5:16 [NKJV], it says, *"Rejoice Always!"* Joy is not reserved for the good times but for the tough times. James 1:2 [NKJV] says this, *"My brethren, count it all joy when you fall into various trials, knowing that the testing of your faith produces patience."*

In Acts 16:16-24, Apostle Paul and Silas were thrown in jail because Paul commanded a demon to leave a slave girl. Before being shackled and thrown in prison, Paul and Silas's clothes were torn off and beaten severely with rods. The Scripture says they had many stripes on them. While they were in jail (see verse 25), they prayed and sang hymns to God. Can you imagine the physical pain and discomfort they were in! They could have chosen to be angry and sad, but instead, being full of the Spirit they were full of joy.

When we have the proper perspective, it is not difficult to experience joy. Paul writes in Romans 8:28 [NKJV] – *"And we know that* **all things work together for good** *to those who love God, to those who are the called according to His purpose."* All things include the good, the bad, and the ugly – it is all working together for your good! Keep this in your heart and mind, and you will experience continuous joy throughout your life.

### Peace

Peace is a gift given to us by Jesus. In John 14:27 [NKJV], Jesus says, *"Peace I leave with you, My peace I give to you; not as the world gives do I give to you. Let not your heart be troubled, neither let it be afraid."*

We also hear of this peace in Philippians 4:7 NKJV, which says, *"and the peace of God, which surpasses all understanding, will guard your hearts and minds through Christ Jesus."* Peace is a guard! When we allow anxiety and fear to come upon us, we have let our guard down. Isaiah 9:6 says that Jesus is the Prince of Peace. As believers who walk in the Spirit, we have Jesus dwelling on the inside of us. That means we are carriers of His peace.

In addition to the peace we have with Jesus, we are commanded to be in peace with one another. The opposite of peace is conflict. If we find ourselves in constant conflict, we can be certain we are not walking in the Spirit. In Hebrews 12:14, the author of Hebrews wrote: *"Pursue peace with all people, and holiness, without which no one will see the Lord."* Notice that peace and holiness are mentioned together in the same statement. That is because holiness is connected to our behavior, and we demonstrate peacefulness by the way we behave.

### **Long-suffering**

Luke 21:19 [NKJV] says, *"By your patience possess your souls."* In other words, when we exercise patience, we are in control of our soul, which includes our emotions. Merriam-Webster's online dictionary defines longsuffering as "patiently enduring lasting offense or hardship.[8]" Some synonyms for "longsuffering" are patient, tolerant, and uncomplaining. Long-suffering does not just indicate how long we have suffered, but rather our response to that suffering – our attitude.

---

8 Merriam-Webster Diction, definition of "long-suffering", https://www.merriam-webster.com/dictionary/long-suffering

In contrast, the antonyms for longsuffering are <u>complaining</u>, <u>fed up</u>, <u>impatient</u>, and <u>protesting</u>. Consider how it makes you feel when you are around someone that complains all the time. Are you that person, perhaps? Philippians 2:14-15 [NKJV] says this, *"Do all things without complaining and disputing, that you may become blameless and harmless, children of God without fault in the midst of a crooked and perverse generation, among whom you shine as lights in the world, holding fast the word of life, so that I may rejoice in the day of Christ that I have not run in vain or labored in vain."*

Notice that <u>we are</u> to do all things without complaining and disputing to remain blameless and harmless without fault. In other words, when we complain and argue, we are blameful, harmful, and full of weakness. Ouch! God hates when we murmur and complain. Numbers 11:1 [NKJV] is one example that shows how much God hates those who complain:

> "Now when the people complained, it displeased the Lord; for the Lord heard it, and His anger was aroused. So the fire of the Lord burned among them, and consumed some in the outskirts of the camp."

Now, thankfully God is not burning us up and killing us when we complain today like He did some of the children of Israel that dreadful day. However, our complaining can kill our hope, destiny and prevent us from receiving anything from the Lord. When we consider all that Jesus suffered, being blameless and without ever having sinned – for Him not to complain on His way to being killed– how dare we complain about issues we face in this world? Isaiah 53:7 [NKJV] says this about Jesus, *"He was oppressed and He was afflicted, yet He opened not His mouth; He was led as a lamb to the slaughter, and as a sheep before its shearers is silent, so He opened not His mouth."*

We are also to endure longsuffering with one another. We all have friends, family, or even co-workers that tend to annoy us. If you have any children, your patience has certainly been tested. Our differences and beliefs set us all on a potential collision course for conflict.

But read what Colossians 3:12-13 [NKJV] instructs us to do – "*Therefore, as the elect of God, holy and beloved, put on tender mercies, kindness, humility, meekness, longsuffering; bearing with one another, and forgiving one another, if anyone has a complaint against another; even as Christ forgave you, so you also must do.*" These verses do not give us any wiggle room, do they!?

Complaining is the primary indicator that we are not walking in the Spirit but operating in the flesh. Since Scripture tells us not to complain, we are sinning in a way that leads to spiritual death if we do it anyway. In the following activity, you will see what else Scripture teaches about longsuffering.

1. Read James 1:2-4. What does it say produces patience? And what happens as a result of having patience? Explain:

_____
_____
_____

2. Read James 5:9. What does it say happens if we complain?

_____
_____

3. Read Romans 5:3-4. What is the benefit of longsuffering?

4. Read Philippians 4:8-9. What should we do instead of complaining?

5. Read Joshua 1:8. What does God instruct us to do? Is it possible to do this and complain at the same time?

Jesus tells us in John 16:33 that we will have tribulations (trouble) in this world, and in this same verse, He tells us to be of good cheer because He has overcome the world. Therefore, let us be careful to obey the Word of God and avoid complaining at all costs. Complaining does not help us; it hinders us.

## Kindness and Goodness

Since these two words are closely related and often used interchangeably, we'll consider them together. It is said that kindness reflects a tender heart, while goodness is the result of kindness. Neither kindness or goodness is circumstantial or situational. We either have this fruit and consistently demonstrate it, or we do not. To see goodness and kindness in action, take a moment now and read Luke 10:30-35 [NKJV]. In verse 33, we see the Samaritan had compassion for the man, which was his kindness. When he bandaged up the injured man's wounds, he was demonstrating goodness. Where else do you see kindness and goodness in this passage of Scripture?

## Faithfulness

To be faithful is to be loyal, steadfast, and trustworthy. When we are faithful, God can trust us to keep our word and do what we say. When we are faithful, we are good stewards, fiercely protecting everything in our care.

 ASSIGNMENT

Stop here and carefully read the Parable of the Talents in Matthew 25:14-30. After reading, answer the following questions:

1. When the man returned from his travels, how did he respond to the servant with five talents? With two talents?

_____
_____
_____
_____

2. As a result of their faithfulness, what happened to the servant with five talents? With the two talents?

_____
_____
_____
_____

3. What did the man call the servant that had the one talent in verse 26, and why?

_____
_____
_____
_____

4. What happens to the unfaithful (unprofitable) according to verse 30?

_____
_____
_____
_____

Just as God is faithful and just to us, He expects no less from us.

**Gentleness**

Another word for gentleness is meekness. The carnal mind confuses gentleness with being weak, but it is not. Proverbs 25:15 NKJV says, *"...And a gentle tongue breaks a bone."* Someone once said that gentleness is strength under control. Some synonyms for the word gentleness are mildness, calmness, tenderness, and softness. The antonyms of gentleness are roughness and harshness, which shouldn't be confused with firm or bold. To the Corinthians, the Apostle Paul says in 1 Corinthians 4:21 [NKJV], *"What do you want? Shall I come to you with a rod, or in love and a spirit of gentleness?"* In other words, he is asking them, "Do you want me to force you to obey, or through gentleness and love, convince you to obey willingly?"

The fruit of gentleness is one of compassion and carefulness. Unfortunately, many well-meaning believers have put a bad taste in people's mouths concerning the things of God because they lack this fruit. Rather than forcing someone to comply and believe what we say, we will win many if we are simply careful in our delivery and demonstrate love.

### **Self-Control**

What is amazing about self-control is mastering it; we conquer the works of the flesh. However, all works of the flesh represent a lack of self-control. The dictionary defines self-control as 'restraint exercised over one's impulses, emotions, or desires.[9]" **Impulses** are sudden responses to people, situations, or circumstances that are ill-considered. An impulsive person lacks wisdom. They make rash decisions based on temporary circumstances, and rash decisions have lasting, unexpected consequences.

**Emotions** are feelings that include happiness, anger, depression, sorrow, fear, love, etc. When we lack self-control, we are led by our

---

9 "Definition of SELF-CONTROL." Www.merriam-Webster.com, www.merriam-webster.com/dictionary/self-control.

emotions rather than by truth and logic. For example, Cain's anger caused him to kill his brother Abel, and Abel didn't even do anything to him! The murder was an impulsive response to an unchecked emotion.

**Desires** are things we crave. We can desire something so badly that we can make bad decisions without self-control, which can be life-altering. Simply put, self-control is self-discipline. We are responsible for controlling our actions. It is not God's job to control our flesh for us. What He has done is given us the gift of grace, which empowers us to operate in self-control.

We are also required to control our thoughts, which also falls under self-control. The devil has no control over our thoughts. We choose what we think. Our emotions, impulses, and desires are empowered by what we think.

 **ASSIGNMENT**

**Read the scriptures below and answer the questions that follow.**

Read Proverbs 25:28. What does it teach us about self-control or the lack thereof?

_____

_____

_____

_____

Read 2 Corinthians 10:5-6. What does it teach us about controlling our thoughts?

_____

_____

_____

_____

Read Ephesians 4:29. What does it teach about self-control?

_____

_____

_____

Read James 1:19-20. What does it have to say about self-control?

_____

_____

_____

Read Philippians 4:8 and Joshua 1:8. What are we controlling in these two verses? How can obeying what's said in Joshua 1:8 help us with self-control?

_____

_____

_____

_____

Read Proverbs 29:11. What does it say about a person who does not have self-control?

NO LONGER A TARE • 59

_____

_____

_____

_____

Read Proverbs 21:23. What does it teach about self-control?

_____

_____

_____

_____

When we are walking in the Spirit, we have no room for the works of the flesh. We are literally surrendering complete control of ourselves and our lives to the Holy Spirit. Take some time to reflect on which fruit you are not consistently producing. Pray and ask the Lord to help you improve in those areas. Remember, He has already given us grace, which He told the Apostle Paul was enough. It is up to you to do the work.

## THE GIFTS OF THE SPIRIT

The Holy Spirit is responsible for the distribution of spiritual gifts. When the Holy Spirit fills a believer, they become candidates to receive any of the spiritual gifts. We cannot earn the right to operate in the gifts, but we can desire spiritual gifts (1 Corinthians 14:1). In 1 Corinthians 12:8-11 [NKJV], it says:

> "for to one is given the <u>word of wisdom</u> through the Spirit, to another the <u>word of knowledge</u> through the same Spirit, to another <u>faith</u> by the same Spirit, to another <u>gifts of healings</u> by the same

Spirit, to another the <u>working of miracles</u>, to another <u>prophecy</u>, to another <u>discerning of spirits</u>, to another different kinds of <u>tongues</u>, to another the <u>interpretation of tongues</u>."

Spiritual gifts are not for us to benefit ourselves but for others. As it states in 1 Peter 4:10, "As each one has received a gift, minister it to one another, as good stewards of the manifold grace of God." Notice that this verse says each one of us has received a gift. That means, at a minimum, every born-again spirit-filled believer has at least one gift but could certainly have more. While spiritual gifts are important and desperately needed for the work of the Lord, our priority should be on cultivating the fruit of the Spirit. When we do not have the fruit of the Spirit, we will not be pure and effective in ministering those gifts to others. Apostle Paul discusses this in 1 Corinthians 13:1-2 [NKJV]:

"Though I speak with the tongues of men and of angels, but have not love, I have become sounding brass or a clanging cymbal. And though I have the gift of prophecy, and understand all mysteries and all knowledge, and though I have all faith, so that I could remove mountains, but have not love, I am nothing."

What this passage also reveals is that we can operate in the gifts of the Spirit, and still not be saved in the end. Why? Because He commands us to love; and if we don't love as He requires, we are disobeying His word. Disobedience disqualifies us from inheriting the Kingdom of God.

As we have seen in 1 Corinthians 12:8-11, there are nine gifts of the Spirit. These nine gifts represent three spiritual categories: Gifts of Revelation, Gifts of Inspiration, and Gifts of Power. Following is a brief description of each spiritual gift.

### Gifts of Revelation
- **The Word of Wisdom** – is a supernatural revelation or insight into God's divine will and purpose for people, problems, or situations that arise. For example, in Genesis 41:1-8, Pharaoh has a disturbing dream, but he could find no one to interpret the dream's meaning. Finally, Joseph is brought before Pharaoh (see Genesis 41:25-32), revealing the dream's interpretation of a severe famine in the coming years.

After Joseph interpreted the dream, he provided a solution, the word of wisdom, necessary to prepare for and survive the famine (see Genesis 41:33-36). Continue reading the rest of the chapter to see how the manifestation of the wisdom began to play out. For further edification, continue reading through chapters 42-45 to see the full manifestation and benefit of this wonderful gift.

The word of wisdom is often used with other spiritual gifts. Take Pharaoh's dream as an example, which was a prophecy. After Joseph gave Pharaoh the prophecy (his dream interpretation), he immediately moved to the gift of the word of wisdom to provide the solution. It would not have been possible for Joseph to come up with the solution to save the people on the earth, and have it play out exactly as he described on his own. This gift is not the wisdom of man, nor this world, but from God.

- **The Word of Knowledge** – is a supernatural revelation of past or present Information about someone or something previously unknown by the person giving the word of knowledge. This gift is often confused with the gift of prophecy, but it is not the same thing. If it is revealed to you that someone is having marital problems and you share it with them, you have not prophesied to them – you have given them a word of knowledge. In John 4:4-17, when Jesus talked with the woman at the well, He told her facts about her life that He could not have known. When Jesus told her how many husbands she had, that was a word of knowledge.

Another example of this gift in action is in Acts 5:1-11. In this account, Ananias and Sapphira sold their property and brought part of the money to the Apostles, leading them to believe that he gave them all of the proceeds. No one told Peter about this; this knowledge was supernaturally revealed to him by God.

As with the word of wisdom, this gift is also used in conjunction with other spiritual gifts, such as prophecy and healing. The Holy Spirit can reveal to you that someone has cancer (word of knowledge), and through the gift of healing, that person's cancer is healed.

- **Discerning of Spirits** – With this gift, the Holy Spirit gives you the ability to discern people's hearts and minds and learn whether they are good or evil. The account of Simon, the Sorcerer in Acts 8:14-23, is a good example. Simon wanted the apostles to sell him the gift of the Holy Spirit. In verse 23, Apostle Peter said to him, "For I see that you are poisoned by bitterness and bound by iniquity." Simon asking to buy the Holy Spirit was wrong, and Peter understood what spirit was in Simon.

Jesus demonstrated this gift many times. One example is found in Matthew 9:1-4 in the account of Jesus healing a paralytic. Notice verse 3 says, *"some of the scribes <u>said within themselves...</u>"*; they did not speak the thought aloud, but Jesus was able to discern what they said anyway.

### Gifts of Inspiration
- **Prophecy** – simply put, is a supernatural utterance. The definition for prophecy in the King James Bible Dictionary says this:
  1. A foretelling; prediction; a declaration of something to come. As God only knows future events with certainty, no being but God or some person informed by Him, can utter a real prophecy;
  2. In Scripture; a book of prophecies;
  3. Preaching; public interpretation of Scripture; exhortation or instruction.[10]

Notice in the first definition that it says prophecy is "a declaration of something to come." While prophecy is not just a prediction, this first definition is most likely when prophecy is discussed. In this context, a supernatural utterance to be considered prophecy has to speak of what has <u>not happened yet,</u> which is the clear distinction between word of knowledge and prophecy. But any declaration on the written Word of God, the prophecy follows the second and third definitions.

- **Different kinds of tongues** (also known as diversities of tongues) are supernatural utterances in other languages that the speaker does not know. For example, in Acts 2:1-12, after the Holy Spirit filled the 120 disciples, they spoke in different languages. But the people, gathered from many nations, understood the Apostles speaking in their language.

These tongues are not to be confused with praying in the Holy Spirit. 1 Corinthians 14:2 [NKJV] says , *"For he who speaks in a*

---

10 "King James Bible Dictionary - Reference List - Prophecy." King James Bible Dictionary, www.kingjamesbibledictionary.com/Dictionary/prophecy. Accessed 25 June 2021.

*tongue does not speak to men but to God, for none understands him; however in the spirit, he speaks mysteries."*

- **Interpretation of tongues** – is the supernatural ability to interpret in the native tongue of other languages not known by the interpreter. To benefit those who hear the tongues, someone must interpret. In 1 Corinthians 14:27-28 [NKJV], it says: *"If anyone speaks in a tongue, let there be two or at the most three, each in turn, and let one interpret. But if there is no interpreter, let him keep silent in church, and let him speak to himself and to God."*

**Gifts of Power**
- **Faith** – is the supernatural ability to believe God without doubt, unbelief, or reasoning. This gift of faith is an unwavering belief in God despite the situation or circumstance. The believer can hold out until the end. A great example of this gift in operation is when God told Abraham to sacrifice his son Isaac (see Genesis 22:1-13). He had to be stopped by the Angel of the Lord from killing Isaac. On the other hand, this gift <u>was not in</u> operation when Peter walked on water because he got scared, doubted, and began to sink (see Matthew 14:25-33).

As with other gifts, this gift is usually paired with other gifts. For example, the gift of faith and the gifts of healing or the gifts of faith and prophecy. It takes the gift of faith for a believer to declare a word of prophecy, especially when it is a word of correction or rebuke.

- **Gifts of healing** – This spiritual gift is supernatural power to heal all manner of sickness without human aid or medicine. There are many examples of the gifts of healing in Scripture. For instance, we read in Acts 3:1-10 the account of a man that was lame from birth who, after taking Apostle Peter's hand, instantly was able to walk, leap and run.

The Holy Spirit does not just give the gifts of healing to apostles, but to anyone He chooses. For example, in Acts 9, Saul (who later became Apostle Paul) was struck blind by Jesus. The Lord sent a disciple named Ananias to heal Saul of his blindness (see verses 17-18).

- **Working of Miracles** – is supernatural power to intervene in the ordinary course of nature and to counteract natural laws. For example, Jesus raised Lazarus from the dead after four days (see John 11:38-44). Also, Moses parts the Red Sea in Exodus 14:10-22.

Miracles are mighty acts and not reduced to trivial things. Other examples of miracles are found in 1 Kings 17:1-7, where Elijah caused the rain to stop, and in Joshua 10:12-15 when the sun and moon stood still. God blesses us in many ways, but we must regard true miracles as miracles and be careful not to categorize anything unexpected that happens as a miracle.

Considering the few miracles that we have reviewed in Scripture, would you consider a bill being paid a miracle? What about getting a job for which you do not qualify? These are lovely blessings – favor even, but in no way do they compare to any of the miracles we see in Scripture.

The Holy Spirit can use anyone to operate in a gift(s), but that does not mean that person is in a ministry office. Let's consider Acts 2:17 [NKJV], which says, *"And it shall come to pass in the last days, says God, that I will pour out My Spirit on all flesh; your sons and your daughters shall prophesy, Your young men shall see visions, Your old men shall dream dreams."* This Scripture did not say, "And My

Prophets shall prophesy, and My Seers shall see visions and dream dreams." As a believer filled with the Holy Spirit, we all qualify to be used by Holy Spirit. The Holy Spirit can use anyone He wants to prophesy, but that does not mean the person is a Prophet.

 **ASSIGNMENT**

**Read the Scripture references below and answer the questions that follow.**

**Read 1 Samuel 19:20-24**

In verse 20, what group of people did Saul's messengers see prophesying?

___

In verse 20, what happened to the messengers of Saul?

___

In verses 23 and 24, who was prophesying? And was he a prophet?

___

**Read Acts 19:1-7**
Who did Apostle Paul find according to verse 1?

What happened when Paul laid his hands on them in verse 6?

Does it say that they became prophets?

The purpose of all spiritual gifts is for the edification of the church and others. Therefore, we must check our motives in wanting to operate in the gifts of the Holy Spirit. In 1 Corinthians 14:12 [NKJV], it says, *"Even so, since you are zealous (eager) for spiritual gifts, let it be for the edification of the church that you seek to excel."*

## **Gifts and Order**

Read and discuss 1 Corinthians 14:26-40 as a group. Here Paul is explaining the importance of order when operating in the gifts of the Spirit. He did not deny their gifts of the Spirit but wanted them to know that responsibility and order would prevent confusion or division.

Some things to consider when operating in the gifts of the Spirit, especially in your local church:

1. We first must understand that Spiritual gifts are necessary for edifying the church.
2. People do not own these gifts; it is not about us or how great we are. It is all about Jesus!
3. Regardless of how the Holy Spirit moves through you, permission from the Pastor or presiding minister is needed for you to operate that gift. If the Holy Spirit reveals something to you or gives you a word of prophecy, you must follow the rules of that church regarding releasing the word. For example, it may be that in all prophetic words, a leader must vet the words before releasing them. Make sure you are obedient to the rules of the house and the desire for order when using your spiritual gifts. Too bad more churches don't have this problem controlling the gifts of the spirit.
4. Rebuking the Pastor or a church leader, even under the guise of "a prophecy," should not be done. Again, God is a God of order. If your leader is in error and the Lord shows it to you, it is for you to pray – not move to rebuke and correct your leader. God will deal with that leader as He sees fit. Your job is to pray.
5. Never "blurt" out a prophetic word during teaching/preaching. Refer back to 1 Corinthians 14:32. In Jeremiah 20:9, Prophet

Jeremiah describes the Word of the Lord like a fire shut up in his bones. If you are gifted to prophesy, you may have a similar experience, but you must hold that fire until the proper time.

6. Performance (theatrics) is a work of the flesh; avoid it at all costs. Meaning it is unnecessary to scream, flip, dance, and shake when giving the word. Just say it.
7. Even outside of the church setting, have your prophetic words vetted (judged) before releasing them. 1 Corinthians 14:29 tells us clearly that prophecy must be judged.

Remember! God is not the author of confusion (1 Cor 14:33).

# MODULE 4

BIBLICAL CHURCH MEMBERSHIP

# BIBLICAL CHURCH MEMBERSHIP

In general, when we think of membership, we automatically begin to think of ways in which we benefit from membership. Some memberships you may be familiar with include "country club memberships, frequent flyer membership programs, gym memberships and the like. We pay a fee or make minimum purchases to get the benefits that these programs offer. Then, if the program benefits do not meet our expectations, we cancel the membership and find another one that will.

Unfortunately, within the church, this concept of membership has been practiced. Within this context, people tend to believe that when they join a church and give their tithes and offerings, the church is supposed to provide them with perks and service in return. In a sense, tithes and offerings are often seen or treated as membership fees. Church membership practiced in this manner is neither Biblical nor spiritual and is not what the Lord had in mind. In his book "I am a Church Member (IACM), Thom Rainer writes:[11]

---

[11] Rainer, Thom S. I Am a Church Member : Discovering the Attitude That Makes the Difference. Nashville, Tenn., B & H Pub. Group, 2013.

"For them, membership is about receiving instead of giving, being served instead of serving, rights instead of responsibilities, and entitlements instead of sacrifices. This wrongful view of membership sees the tithes and offerings as membership dues that entitle members to a never-ending list of privileges and expectations, instead of an unconditional cheerful gift to God."

Consider for a moment your expectations of your local church. What do you think the relationship should be like between you and your church? What are the expectations of your church? Discuss as a group before continuing.

## **A CALL TO SERVE**

We are members of Christ's Body, and as His body, we are called to serve. 1 Corinthians 12:12 says, *"For as the body is one and has many members, but all the members of that one body, being many, are <u>one body</u>, so also is Christ."* Put another way, as born-again believers, we are individual members, but collectively, we are a single body. In verses 15-21 of that same chapter, Apostle Paul begins to describe the parts of the physical body and the importance of each part (hand, eye, foot, etc.), and he likens it to the Body of Christ.

Just as each of our physical body parts have a job to do, so do we, as members of Christ's body and members of our church. The brain thinks; the eyes see; the nose smells; the teeth chew; the fingers touch, hold and grab; the feet walk; the legs hold up the body; and the skin protects the organs – you get the picture. Every part of the body benefits from and relies on the work of the other body parts. So what does this have to do with church membership? Everything! We are to serve one another, not be served like some members of an elite club. In Matthew 20:28 [ NKJV], Jesus says, *"Just as the Son of Man did not come to be served, but to serve, and to give His life a ransom for many."* Are we greater than Christ, that we can receive the services of others, but not do our part in serving?

When you join a church, there are some expectations of service. Therefore, people who only attend worship services or church events but do not volunteer or serve should be considered visitors rather than members.

 **ASSIGNMENT**

**Review each of the Scripture references below and write down what each says about serving.**

Read 1 Peter 4:10 and write what it says about serving. Who should serve in this verse?

_____

_____

_____

_____

Read Colossians 3:23-24. What does it say about serving, and who are we serving as unto?

_____

_____

_____

_____

Read John 13:12-13. Who is serving whom, and what is Jesus teaching about service?

Read 1 Corinthians 10:24. According to this verse, whose needs are we to consider first above our own?

_____

_____

_____

_____

Just as discussed regarding spiritual gifts, our motives must be pure when serving. We do not serve to be seen or to receive praises from people. Most churches will provide a list of some sort to their members, listing all the areas in the church where they can serve. When presented with a list of serving opportunities in the past, how did you decide where to help? Was it based on what seemed fun, exciting, or recognizable? Did you choose that area to serve based on your interests and aspirations? Now be honest with yourself and God. A person with a pure servant's heart will ask, "where is the greatest need, and how may I serve there?" The opportunity to serve in areas that interest you will always be there, but the needs of others should always come before your preferences.

One of the gifts not covered was the gift of helps, which is incredibly vital in the proper function of any church. Remember the discussion on the Body of Christ and how it relates to a physical body. Let us examine the toenail for a moment. At first glance, it does not appear to do much, and it doesn't look all that exciting. But rip that toenail off, and the rest of the body will feel it!

In addition to people who do not want to serve, some serve too much – meaning in too many areas. Doing too much will cause what you are doing to lack in some way. Before serving on multiple teams, consider the time and commitment of each to ensure nothing goes lacking, including your spiritual health and well-being. It is never the desire of true church leaders for those serving to become weary and spiritually malnourished. Remember, always find out where the greatest need lies first and begin faithfully serving there.

## **COMMITMENT**

As we begin this discussion on committing to the church, we must understand that our highest commitment is to God. If we are not fully committed to God, we will not understand or value committing to His church. In other words, our failure to commit to the church is a direct reflection of our commitment to God. Jesus says in Matthew 22:37-38 [NKJV], *"You shall love the Lord your God with all your heart, with all of your soul, and with all of your mind."* Jesus was not just referencing emotion but to a level of responsibility and dedication to God. There is a yoke and a burden to being committed to God; to be His bondservant, Matthew 11:30 reminds us that His yoke is easy, and His burden is light.

Oxford Dictionary defines commitment as "a promise to do something or to behave in a particular way; a promise to support somebody/ something; the fact of committing yourself."[12] To further clarify commitment, some synonyms include "pledge, engagement, responsibil-

---

12 "Commitment Noun - Definition, Pictures, Pronunciation and Usage Notes | Oxford Advanced Learner's Dictionary at OxfordLearnersDictionaries.com." Www.

ity, need, promise, guarantee, duty, word, undertaking, charge, vow, must, devoir, committal, ought."[13]  So it certainly doesn't look like there is a lot of wiggle room when steadfast commitment is involved.

Now how does this translate into serving in our local churches?  When you join a local church, you make a vow to be a faithful, committed, and fruitful member – providing stability and not a burden.  Too often, people treat God's church as an optional thing to do as they have time and if they feel like it.  What if God treated us this way?

**Review and discuss the following as a group.**

Why do you believe the commitment level for our jobs and families is far greater than our commitment to the church?
Read Acts 2:42-47.  Does this church look anything like the church today?
How do you think God feels about the online church (instead of in-person gatherings)?  Can that be considered "assembling yourselves" as mentioned in Hebrews 10?

## **GROWING IN UNITY**

Jesus prays for us in John 17:20-23 [NKJV]: *"I do not pray for these alone, but also for those who will believe in Me through their word; that they all may be one, as You, Father, are in Me, and I in You; that they also may be one in Us, that the world may believe that You sent Me. And the glory which You gave Me I have given them, that they may be one just as We are one; I in them, and You in Me; that*

---

oxfordlearnersdictionaries.com, www.oxfordlearnersdictionaries.com/definition/english/commitment?q=commitment. Accessed 25 June 2021

13 "The Definition of Commitment." Www.dictionary.com, 2019, www.dictionary.com/browse/commitment.

*they may be perfect in one, and the world may know that You have sent Me, and have loved them as You have loved Me."*

In His prayer, Jesus offers the following reasons for wanting us united:
1. That as we are one (united), we become one in Him and the Father
2. That the world may <u>believe</u> that God sent Jesus
3. That we would receive His glory that God gave Him
4. That we may be perfect
5. And lastly, that the world may <u>know</u> that God sent Jesus and that God has loved us, just as God loves Jesus.

Reading this prayer should make all of us want to go above and beyond to ensure we are doing our part in unifying with one another. Considering again that we are the Body of Christ and how it relates to the physical body – can you imagine body pieces spread out all over the place? Sounds gross, doesn't it?

In 1 Corinthians 1:10, Apostle Paul pleads with the church of Corinth concerning unity:

"Now I plead with you, brethren, by the name of our Lord Jesus Christ, that you all speak the same thing, and there be no divisions among you, but that you be perfectly joined together in the same mind and in the same judgment."

Scripture commands us to be united. Jesus is coming back for a bride, not brides.

We will now cover several ways to ensure we are fulfilling the Lord's prayer request for us to be united.

### **Mark those that cause division**

Romans 16:17 [NKJV] says, *"Now I urge you, brethren, note those who cause divisions and offenses, contrary to the doctrine which you learned, and avoid them. For those who are such do not serve our Lord Jesus Christ...."*

Two main points revealed in this Scripture:
1) We are to avoid, not join, those that cause division.
2) Those that cause division DO NOT serve Jesus.

Now more than ever, there is great division in the universal church. The bulk of division stems from doctrinal beliefs and socio-cultural issues. While we cannot force unity across the universal church, we can do our part by walking in unity in our local churches.

 **ASSIGNMENT**

**Read the following case study and answer the questions that follow.**

Bill and George are members of the same church, they both serve in some capacity, and they faithfully give their tithes and offerings. One day, Bill and George had an argument that led to them no longer speaking to each other. Bill begins to tell different members in the church about how George wronged him. As a result, some of the members look at George differently, and some of them start to avoid George, and they too begin to tell others what Bill shared with them concerning George.

Based on what we have discussed about division, answer the following questions:

1. Bill is an active member of the church, and he gives faithfully. Now considering his behavior and what we read in Romans 16:17, does Bill serve Jesus?
2. When Bill told the other members about his problem with George, what should the other members have done?
3. Some of those members told others in the church what George allegedly did to Bill – are they guilty of causing division? Do they serve Jesus?
4. Read Proverbs 6:16-19. What does it say about those who cause division and how God feels about them?

**<u>Defeating the Spirit of Offense</u>**

Jesus said in Luke 17:1 [NKJV], *"…It is impossible that no offenses should come, but woe to him through whom they do come!"* Jesus let us know that there is no way to avoid offenses; He said it was impossible. Offenses have caused people to leave churches, and in some cases, to leave the faith. This section will discuss ways to recognize and deal with offenses quickly to be a unified body as Christ desires.

If we act as instructed in Philippians 4:8-9 [NKJV,] we will not have an issue handling offense appropriately. Here is what it says:

> "Finally, brethren, whatever things are true, whatever things are noble, whatever things are just, whatever things are pure, whatever things are lovely, whatever things are of good report, if there is any virtue and if there is anything praiseworthy – meditate on these things. The things which you learned and received and heard and saw in me, these do, and the God of peace will be with you."

Offenses start with a thought. To be offended is a decision we make in our minds. Since our thoughts craft our behavior, we must be diligent in guarding our minds and thinking pure thoughts, regardless of the situation or circumstance. Offenses are viruses that spread, polluting our soul. It clouds our thoughts, affects our hearing, impacts our emotions, and in many cases, causes health issues that take root from the unresolved offense.

The spirit of offense does not settle in alone. It brings with it pride, rejection, insecurity, and a host of other demonic spirits. It is an extremely dangerous spirit sent by the enemy to destroy God's people and bring division.

 **ASSIGNMENT**

**Read the following Scriptures and write what they say about offense:**

Acts 24:16.

_____
_____
_____

Proverbs 18:19.

_____
_____
_____

Proverbs 19:11.

_____
_____

**Read Acts 15:36-41, and then discuss the following questions as a group.**

1. Paul was offended by Barnabus for insisting that John Mark go with them. Was Paul wrong for not wanting John Mark to go? Was it that big of a deal?
2. What could have been done differently by either Paul or Barnabus?
3. What kind of example do you think was set for Mark and Silas in the middle of this dispute?
4. Was the issue worth them splitting up?
5. Have you had a similar dispute with a fellow church member that caused a split? Looking back on it now, would you have done anything differently?

Offense does not always come as the result of an argument or disagreement. Many times, it is the result of a person having a wrong perspective. Unfortunately, some people wear glasses called "offense." They are always looking for an opportunity to be offended. When they interact with people, everything they hear and see is filtered through their 'offense lenses.' They're always the victim of a misunderstanding or mistreatment. As mentioned earlier, people leave churches because of offense. Look at some of the reasons why Christians become offended and often leave the church:

- The Pastor did not shake their hand or speak to them on a given day.
- Someone else did not speak to them.
- They auditioned to be on the worship team but did not get accepted.

- They interviewed for a position in the church but did not get it.
- The Pastor's sermon was talking about them.
- They were removed from serving or leading a team.
- No one called them when they were out sick.
- The Pastor did not visit them or their family members in the hospital.
- They were not officially recognized for a good deed.
- Someone else's name was called, but theirs was not.
- The church did not officially recognize their birthday.
- The Children's church staff removed their children for misbehaving.
- They believe the leadership is showing favoritism toward others.
- They're rebuked for doing something wrong or for not doing something right.

This list could go on for several more pages, but you likely get the point. Notice that the focus was on the <u>person</u> and how <u>they</u> felt or how <u>they perceived</u> treatment. Me, myself, and I are constants in this person's vocabulary, instead of "we, us, and our." It is impossible to be unified when we are always concerned without ourselves.

In addition to those who are easily offended or look for offense, some people take on other people's offenses. In the previous case with Bill and George, this is what happened. Bill shared his offense about George with others, who then became offended and told still more. No matter how close you are to a person, you can never be sure unless you witness the issue first-hand. When someone is bringing a problem to you, it is supposed to be for restoration – not to get you on their side; and only when both parties are present should the matter be discussed. Let's review a Biblical example of how we should handle offenses. In Matthew 18:15-17 [NKJV], Jesus says:

"Moreover, if your brother sins against you, go and tell him his fault between you and him along. If he hears you, you have gained your brother. But if he will not hear, take with you one or two more, that 'by the mouth of two or three witnesses every word may be established.' And if he refuses to hear them, tell it to the church. But if he refuses even to hear the church, let him be to you like a heathen and a tax collector."

The steps to dealing with the offense that we see in this passage are:
1. Talk to the person that offended you, preferably face to face and in private.
2. If you can resolve the issue between the two of you, it should end there. No one else needs to know about it. However, if the person is complex and does not want to work with you, you must involve one or two other people. It is best if a neutral party is requested to mediate, or the person will automatically assume they are biased.
3. If the person still refuses to work through the issue, even after the one or two witnesses/mediators try to reason with them, you bring it before church leadership.

If we followed Jesus' instructions for dealing with an offense, we would have a higher restoration rate, and there would be greater unity in the church. Think back to times where you were offended by someone. Consider what we have discussed; would you have handled the situation differently? If you are easily offended, consider these steps to defeat the spirit of offense.

1. When you find yourself offended by someone, ask the following questions:
   a. What are the facts?
   b. What assumptions have I made regarding this situation? What's in my head versus what was said?

    c. If offended by something someone said, consider if what the person said was true.

    d. Why did this bother me so much?

Consider the answers to the questions and decide if you are overreacting or genuinely wronged and need to address the offender.

2. Go to the person that offended you and explain to them how it made you feel. Remember the instructions that Jesus gave us in Matthew 18:15-19. What the person most likely will say to you is, "I'm sorry, I didn't mean to offend you," or "I didn't mean it the way it came across," or "Wow, I had no idea; please forgive me." Receive their apology and move on.

3. Forgive the offense. Consider that you have offended God with your sin, yet He forgave you. Think about all of the bad things you've done in life – not to condemn yourself with, but to be filled with gratitude knowing that you have offended God for most of your life, yet He has forgiven you, and He loves you with an everlasting love.

4. Seek counseling from a Christian counselor or minister. Receiving counseling is a wise and brave step for Christians to take. In most cases, it is difficult for people to identify the root cause of why they are easily offended on their own. Skilled counselors and ministers, full of the Spirit, will play a key role in helping you get to the bottom of your issue and overcome it.

People are easily offended because they do not deal with the offense. Rehearsing an offense in your mind, with no resolution, will keep you in a state of misery. It can pollute your soul to the point of separating you from God.

## **Unity Requires Forgiveness**

When people are offended, they may feel justified in not forgiving the offender, depending on the circumstances. Scripture does not allow us to opt-out of forgiving someone based on the situation. Yes, people have unintentionally and even purposely hurt others emotionally or physically. However, according to Scripture, we must forgive others if we want God to forgive our sins. In Matthew 6:14-15 [NKJV], Jesus says, *"For if you forgive men their trespasses, your heavenly Father will also forgive you. But if you do not forgive men their trespasses, neither will your Father forgive your trespasses."* Yes, Jesus was clear on this, and He also demonstrated this forgiveness Himself. Having never sinned, He was blameless but viciously beaten, nailed to a cross, and in excruciating pain; He still forgave His offenders and prayed that the Father would forgive them as well. (Luke 23:33-34)

When you think about what Jesus went through and the fact that He was able to forgive, do you think He would be willing to hear your reason for not forgiving someone who has hurt and offended you?

 **ASSIGNMENT**

In the Parable of the Unforgiving Servant, Jesus explains the seriousness of forgiveness. Read Matthew 18:21-35 and discuss as a group. Discuss the following questions:

1. Who does the Master represent in this parable, and who does the servant represent?

_____

_____

_____

2.   What does verse 27 reflect?

_____
_____
_____
_____

3.   What happened to the servant in verse 34? What does his punishment represent for us today?

_____
_____
_____
_____

4.   What was the reason for the punishment?

_____
_____
_____
_____

Take a moment and think of anyone you have not forgiven. It could have been a spouse who cheated on you? A family member who violated one of your children? It could be a friend who betrayed you? Maybe someone who stole from you? If you have not forgiven them, do so now or risk losing the gift of salvation.

## UNDERSTANDING HONOR

There are many definitions for the word honor, but the simplest explanation is "to regard or treat someone with admiration and respect." So, at minimum, not considering a person's status or title, we all are supposed to at least respect each other. Craig Groeschel says, "Honor is a gift that you give freely." No one should have to earn the honor.

There can be an entire course on the topic of "honor" alone, but in this section, we will touch on just a few things that will help us understand how we honor God, one another, and those in authority (specifically our leaders).

**Honoring God**

If we do not understand the importance of honoring God, we will not truly understand the importance of honoring others. There is one verse in Scripture that sums up honoring God. In Matthew 22:37 [NKJV], Jesus says, *"Love the Lord your God with all your heart and with all your soul and with all your mind."* The question is, how do we do what Jesus is commanding us to do? The complete and simple answer is – **OBEY HIS WHOLE WORD!** That's right, the whole Word, and not just the easy parts. Obeying the Word of God covers honoring Him.

His Word says –
- to be holy, for He is holy. 1 Peter 1:6
- to repent and be converted. Acts 3:19
- to flee sexual immorality. 1 Cor 6:18
- our body belongs to Him, and to glorify Him in it. 1 Cor 6:19-20
- to honor our word by doing what we say we will do. Matthew 5:37

- to be kind and to forgive one another.  Ephesians 4:32
- walk after the Spirit and not fulfill the lusts of the flesh. Galatians 5:16
- to freely give (includes time and money).  2 Cor 9:6-8
- to serve one another.  1 Peter 4:10

In just these few Scripture references above, we see in His Word that we are to honor Him in all things and all of our ways:  in our bodies, with our time, with our talents, with our hearts, with our money, with our obedience!!!   When we neglect or refuse to do what God tells us to do in His Word, we dishonor Him.  Make a conscious decision today to obey what God says in His Word.  By doing so, we honor Him as he requests and deserves to be honored.

<u>HONORING OTHERS</u>

Under this category, we will cover two people groups: our parents and all others.  Regarding honoring our parents, the Word of God says this in Exodus 20:12 [NKJV], *"Honor your father and your mother, that your days may be long upon the land which the Lord your God is giving you."* Thus, God connects long life with honoring your parents.  Why is this important?  We can serve faithfully, give our time and money generously, feed the poor, avoid sinful acts, etc., but completely miss the mark by dishonoring our parents.

Another reason why this is important is Gods' purpose for your life is for your whole life. Notice that the Word did not say honor your parents if they were good to you or are believers in Jesus  – we are to honor them regardless. But if you dishonor your parents, and your life is cut short by 15 or 20 years, you will fail to fulfill the call of God on your life.

Regarding honoring all others, 1 Peter 2:17 [NKJV] says we should honor all people, not just those we feel are honorable. Honoring others becomes easy when we consider the instruction given in Philippians 2:3-4, which says, *"Let nothing be done through selfish ambition or conceit, but in lowliness of mind let each esteem others better than himself. Let each of you look out not only for his own interests, but also for the interests of others."*

Echoing the same sentiments as Philippians, Romans 12:10 [NKJV] states, *"Be kindly affectionate to one another with brotherly love, in honor giving preference to one another."* We can review many other verses that will support what we have already read, but the bottom line is to honor others. We will have to learn to put other people before ourselves. Honoring others requires us to have a spirit of humility. If we struggle with putting others first, it is an indication that we are dealing with a spirit of pride, which is the opposite of humility.

As a group, discuss ways in which we can consider others above ourselves. How can we put this into practice?

## GIVING

We are made in the image and likeness of God, and as His offspring we are required to pattern ourselves after Him and His ways. Acts 17:25 NKJV declares that God gives to all life, breath, and all things. His gift to the world, every living being within it, is the gift of life. As reviewed early in this guide, He also gives us the gift of salvation. Considering these two gifts (life and salvation), we attain that our God is extraordinarily generous. As such, He expects us to be just like Him.

In an earlier module we covered spending quality time with God, therefore we will not cover it again in this section. What we will cover in this section, are the ways in which we are expected to give.

**<u>Giving of Our Spiritual Gifts</u>**

Romans 12:6-9 KJV states, *"Having then gifts differing according to the grace that is given to us, let us use them: if prophecy, let us prophesy in proportion to our faith; or ministry, let us use it in our ministering; he who teaches, in teaching; he who exhorts, in exhortation; he who gives, with liberality; he who leads, with diligence; he who shows mercy, with cheerfulness."*

The first thing to note from this passage, is that each of us is graced with a gift from God. As we have freely received these spiritual gifts, we are to freely give the benefit of these gifts to others. There are settings and situations where it is appropriate to attach a monetary value to a ministry service or to benefit from a spiritual gift that someone has. Christian counseling, schools of ministry, conferences and seminars are all examples of situations where it is appropriate to charge a fee. When someone is spending hours of their time in counseling and mentoring there should be an agreed upon fee for service. Conferences and seminars usually have costs associated with the events, so again, it would be appropriate to charge a fee. In this teaching, we will specifically focus on freely giving our gifts outside of the exceptions mentioned.

Prophecy was the first gift mentioned in Romans 12:6. We covered earlier that prophecy is a gift given by God. We did not do anything to earn the gift of prophecy, so we have no right to charge people to receive a prophecy from us. Unfortunately, in today's church, there are many who "sell" prophecies, but of course they don't describe it as selling. In some ministry settings, people are sometimes instructed to stand in a line with money, awaiting their turn to receive a "prophecy" from the speaker. Some will not agree with this assessment, but in such settings, people are paying to receive a prophecy, but this should not be so. We are not to buy or sell the gifts of God.

If you've been in the church for some time, you may have heard others teach that we should always bring a gift to a Prophet to receive from him or her. The scripture passage often referenced to support this doctrine can be found in 1 Samuel Chapter 9, where Saul (before being anointed King), was trying to find his father's donkeys. The servant that accompanied Saul on his journey to find the donkeys told him about Samuel the Prophet; explaining to him how everything he says comes to pass (see verse 6), and that he could tell them which way they should go to find the donkeys. Saul liked the idea but wanted to bring something to the Prophet. What you'll notice in verse 7, is that the first thing Saul considered giving Samuel was some bread, but they were all out – he then said, "and there is no present to bring to the man of God. What do we have?" (1 Samuel 9:7 NKJV).

The very last option they considered, after realizing they had nothing else to give him, was one-fourth of a shekel of silver. The point being made here is that money wasn't the first, nor only option considered for blessing the man of God. Nor did the servant mention that Samuel charged a specific fee for prophecy. We should want to give to one another; that is what was demonstrated with Saul and his servant regarding being a blessing to Samuel.

There are two additional points to note from this passage of Scripture. The first point is that God had already told Samuel the day before that he was going to meet Saul. He told Samuel that he had chosen Saul to reign over His people and deliver them from the Philistines (see 1 Samuel 9:15-17 NKJV). This was extremely important to God, especially since His people were crying out to Him.

Now, do you think that Samuel would have withheld the prophecy from Saul if he didn't have money to give him? Of course not. Never give anyone money for a prophecy. If there is something that God wants you to know, He will make sure you get the message for free.

The second and final point is that Samuel also gave to Saul. In verses 22-24, Samuel took Saul and his servant to a hall for them to have dinner with him. They sat in seats of honor and ate the best portion of food that was available (Samuel had it set aside specifically for them). The take-away here is that no matter who someone is or what position they hold, none of us are exempt from giving to one another.

When it comes to ministering our gifts to one another, money should be the last thing on our mind. Whenever and wherever possible, be ready and willing to share the gift that was bestowed on you by God. We reviewed the importance of serving in our local churches. Can you imagine if every minister, usher, exhorter, or teacher received financial compensation for using their gifts in their church? It would be unreasonable to expect such a thing.

## **Giving of Our Time**

Giving our time to the work of the ministry and to one another, is crucial to the advancing of the Kingdom of God. Scriptures provides evidence of this in the book of Acts:

> [Acts 2:41-43 NKJV] Then those who gladly received his word were baptized; and that day about three thousand souls were added to them. And they continued steadfastly in the apostles' doctrine and fellowship, in the breaking of bread, and in prayers. Then fear came upon every soul, and many wonders and signs were done through the apostles.

This passage of scripture in Acts describes the birth of the church after Jesus ascended and the disciples (one-hundred and twenty including the 12 Apostles) were all filled with the Holy Spirit. Peter had just finished preaching the gospel to those that were gathered in Jerusalem and three thousand souls were saved that day. As stated in the scripture, they remained together, fellowshipping, praying and being taught the gospel. Notice in verse 44 it says that they were together and had all things in common. What a beautiful picture of the first church.

When believers spend their time together in unity, others are drawn, souls are saved, and the Kingdom advances. In today's church, things are quite different than what was established in Acts as the model church. The believers that were part of the church in Acts were together daily. Today, church gatherings are limited to once or twice a week, and in most cases the gathering times are short, ranging anywhere from forty-five means to two hours. Congregants are often seen checking the time on their watches or other devices, in hopes that the church service will end soon. What happened? Why is the church today so different from the first church? Can we really expect to receive the same results as the Acts church did when we spend so little time together? (Discuss these questions as a group)

## **Giving of our Finances**

Malachi 3:8 declares that we are guilty of robbing God when we withhold our tithes and offerings. When we consider the reason for tithes and offerings, those of us that belong to God should willingly give finances to help support the work of the ministry. In Malachi 3:10 NKJV God states, *"Bring all the tithes into the storehouse, that there may be food in My house, and try Me now in this."* Says the Lord of Hosts, *"If I will not open for you the windows of heaven and pour out for you such blessing that there will not be room enough to receive it."* God doesn't just expect for us to give our tithes and offerings – He wants us to expect to receive blessings from Him (in return) for obeying Him in giving.

When we tithe, we are not 'paying' for anything. As discussed earlier, tithes and offerings should not be viewed as, or treated as membership fees that we give to our local church to attend meetings there. Rather, when we give tithes and offerings, we are giving it unto the Lord for the work of the ministry. Before proceeding, consider for a moment your local church and all the expenses it has. First, you have the costs associated with the actual church building. Many churches do not have the resources to purchase a building, so many church leaders are responsible for paying monthly mortgages or leases for the building alone.

There are many other recurring costs including electricity, water, gas, and insurance that must be paid. Think for a moment about who should carry the financial burden of operating a church/ministry. Should church leaders' foot the bill on their own? Should they really be expected to pay bills for their own personal homes and families, and pay all the bills for the church as well? Really consider this when you hear people tell you that giving tithes and offering is unnecessary.

Bottom line, the church needs money in order to operate. This is what God meant in Malachi 3:10 when He said, "bring all the tithes and offering…so that there may be food in My house." If there isn't a continuous flow of tithes and offerings being sowed into the church (the House of God), then the church cannot be sustained, and the work of the ministry that is supposed to be conducted in and through that church, will have to cease.

At a high level, we've reviewed the basic expenses that most churches have. Now, consider your Pastor or other ministerial leader that is over the church. They must be available to prepare for and conduct services multiple times a week and be available as often as possible to counsel and attend to the various needs of the congregation. The point being made here, is that your church or ministry leader should receive financial compensation for their role. Many churches also have other staff members to pay as well for their time and expertise, especially if they are working in the ministry in lieu of having another job to support their families.

Unfortunately, there are numerous sermons, books and videos out there that teach against giving tithes and offering. What most of them are proclaiming is that tithing was under the law, and since we are no longer under the law, but rather under grace, we are free from the 'curse' of having to give tithes and offering. As you have learned, or will learn as you study scripture, the law (also known as "The Law of Moses"), was not given to the nation of Israel until Exodus chapter 20. This was after God called Moses to lead the Israelites out of Egypt where they were enslaved for over 400 years. However, we see the first mention of tithing in the Book of Genesis (several generations before Moses was even born). Abram (who later became Abraham) tithed to Melchizedek, who was the king of Salem and the priest of God (see Genesis 14:18-20 NKJV). The fact that Abram (Abraham) tithed before there was even a law, refutes the argument that tithing was initiated and limited to the time of the law.

 **ASSIGNMENT**

**Complete the following Exercise**

1. Read Luke 6:38. Explain what Jesus says about giving and what we can expect as a result.

_____

_____

_____

_____

2. Read 2 Corinthians 9:6. Explain what it teaches about giving, and the importance of 'how' we give.

_____

_____

_____

_____

3. Read Luke 10:3-7. In this passage of scripture, Jesus was sending the disciples out to minister the gospel in various cities. What does He tell them about receiving from those whose house they enter? Jesus refers to the disciples as laborers. What does He say they are worthy of?

_____

_____

_____

_____

4. Read Proverbs 3:9-10. Explain what it teaches about giving.

5. Read Hebrews 10:24-25. What does it teach regarding the saints gathering? What about the frequency?




6. Read Acts 8:14-22. What was Simon trying to purchase? And what was said about him because of it?

# ABOUT THE AUTHOR

Cassandra L. Valentine, an apostle of God, is a dynamic Kingdom leader, teacher, mentor, and trainer. She boldly and unapologetically declares the authentic Word of God, free of personal bias and opinion. God has commissioned her to train, develop and release five-fold ministry leaders to do the work of the ministry, fulfill the individual mandate upon their lives, and do their part in advancing the Kingdom of God. She understands the importance of sending others out rather than keeping them confined to the four walls of their local church body.

As one of Christ Jesus' ambassadors, she is on a mission to prepare the Ecclesia to reign with Christ Jesus on earth, and in the Kingdom of Heaven.

She is a defender of truth and righteousness and is not afraid to confront humanism, false doctrine, and cultural ideologies that plague the Body of Christ. Her commission extends to restoring order within the church and ensuring God acquires and retains His rightful place in His people's hearts, minds, and lives.

Apostle Cassandra is the Founder and CEO of CVM&S, which offers a wide range of services, including ministry consulting, mentorship, training, and spiritual counsel. She is the Founder and Senior Leader of Apostolic Kingdom Builders – a church located in Dallas, Texas.

In addition to her ministry and business endeavors, she is a wife and mother of four. At the time of this publication, her triplets Naomi, Joshua, and Victoria are ten-years old. Her oldest daughter Camillia Valentine, also serves as a Pastor in their church. Her husband, Paul Valentine Sr., serves alongside her, and is a Pastor of Apostolic Kingdom Builders. They have been happily married since April 1991.

**Apostle Cassandra Valentine**
www.toadvancethekingdom.com
**Email**: admin@toadvancethekingdom.com

# INDEX

## A

Abel, 57
accomplish, 41
admiration, 87
Adoration, 36
adultery, 22
adversaries, 10
affections, 32
afflicted, 51
afflictions, 29
afraid, 49, 98
ambassadors, 98
America, 30
Ananias, 26, 61, 64
Angel, 64
anger, 51, 56, 57
animals, 15
annoy, 52
apology, 19, 84
Apostle Paul, 14, 15, 38, 41, 49, 56, 59, 60, 64, 66, 72, 77
Apostle Peter, 62, 64

apostles, 62, 64, 92
Apostolic Kingdom Builders, 99
argument, 23, 78, 81
author, 8, 43, 50, 69, 98
authority, 43, 87

B

baptism, 14, 38, 39
baptized, 6, 14, 38, 92
Barnabus, 81
behaviors, 4, 22
believe, 4, 6, 8, 13, 14, 17, 21, 35, 38, 56, 62, 64, 71, 76, 77, 82
believer, 9, 13, 15, 19, 31, 39, 40, 41, 59, 60, 64, 65
benefits, 1, 39, 40, 41, 71, 72
betrayed, 86
Bible, 18, 20, 21, 23, 32, 33, 35, 40, 42, 62, 63
birthday, 82
blameful, 51
blameless, 29, 51, 85
blessed, 25
blessing, 91, 94
blindness, 64
bold, 56
bondage, 17
bondservant, 75
brethren, 6, 49, 77, 78, 79
bride, 77
burden, 75, 76
business endeavors, 99

C

Cain, 57
camp, 51
Cassandra L. Valentine, 98
cheer, 53
cheerfulness, 90
Christ, 3, 4, 7, 8, 9, 14, 15, 16, 21, 26, 34, 38, 39, 41, 42, 43, 47, 48, 50, 51, 52, 72, 73, 74, 77, 78, 79, 98
Christian, 1, 30, 84
church, 14, 15, 23, 41, 64, 67, 68, 69, 71, 72, 73, 74, 75, 76, 77, 78, 79, 81, 82, 83, 98
citizenship, 1
comforted, 21
commitment, 75, 76
communication, 34
compassion, 54, 56
compensation, 92, 95
complaining, 51, 53
condemnation, 21, 42, 43
condemned, 6, 14
conditions, 5, 21
Conferences, 90
confession, 6
conflict, 50, 52
confusion, 29, 67, 69
Congregants, 93
consequence, 12
converted, 6, 19, 40, 87
correction, 64
counseling, 84, 90
counselors, 84
covenant, 10, 17
Creator, 25, 29, 40
crooked, 51

# D

dangerous, 13, 80
death, 1, 4, 6, 14, 16, 19, 21, 46, 52
decisions, 30, 56, 57
deeds, 6, 22, 47
demon, 49
demonic realm, 13
demonic spirits, 80
depression, 49, 56
destiny, 51
devil, 13, 19, 57
devotional life, 33
dinner, 92
disciples, 7, 34, 38, 63
discontentment, 49
disobedience, 2, 9, 19, 46
dispute, 13, 81
disrespectful, 33
division, 43, 67, 78, 79, 80
divisions, 77, 78
doctrinal beliefs, 78
doubt, 64
dream, 60, 61, 65

# E

edification, 61, 67
electricity, 94
Elijah, 65
emotions, 27, 34, 50, 56, 57, 80
empowering, 47

envy, 22, 48
error, 14, 41, 42, 68
eternal, 1, 13, 14, 22
evil, 22, 29, 48, 62
excuse, 14
exhorter, 92
expenses, 94, 95
eyes, 2, 4, 31, 72
Eyes, 3

F

faith, 2, 13, 35, 38, 40, 49, 59, 60, 64, 79
faithfulness, 47, 55
families, 76
famine, 61
father, 13, 29, 88
favoritism, 82
fear, 9, 23, 50, 56
fee, 71, 90, 91
fellowship, 34, 92, 99
five-fold ministry leaders, 98
flesh, 2, 3, 4, 6, 7, 16, 21, 22, 23, 42, 43, 46, 47, 52, 56, 57, 59, 65, 68, 88
foretelling, 62
forgive, 84, 85, 88
forgiveness, 1, 2, 36, 85
forgiving, 52, 85
formula, 34
fornication, 22
fruit, 7, 8, 13, 47, 54, 56, 59, 60

G

gentleness, 47, 55, 56
gift, 5, 21, 39, 47, 49, 57, 60, 61, 62, 64, 65, 68, 72, 74, 86, 87, 89, 90, 91, 92
gifts, 13, 59, 60, 64, 67, 68, 74, 89, 90, 91, 92
Gifts of Inspiration, 60, 62
Gifts of Power, 60, 64
Gifts of Revelation, 60
Giving, 9, 89, 90, 92, 93
glory, 22, 76, 77
God, 1, 2, 3, 4, 5, 6, 9, 10, 11, 13, 14, 15, 16, 17, 18, 19, 20, 21, 22, 23, 25, 26, 27, 28, 29, 31, 32, 33, 34, 35, 36, 37, 39, 40, 41, 42, 43, 44, 46, 47, 48, 49, 50, 51, 52, 53, 54, 55, 56, 57, 60, 61, 62, 63, 64, 65, 68, 69, 72, 74, 75, 76, 77, 79, 80, 84, 85, 87, 88, 89, 90, 91, 92, 93, 94, 95, 98, 99
goodness, 47, 54
government, 26
grace, 7, 10, 15, 16, 17, 21, 41, 47, 57, 59, 60
gratitude, 84
grieving, 29
guidelines, 18
gym, 71

H

Hannah, 35
happiness, 56
hardship, 50
harshness, 56
healthy, 25
heart, 4, 6, 13, 15, 17, 26, 31, 32, 35, 36, 44, 49, 54, 74, 75, 87
heathen, 83
heaven, 13, 25

heavenly language, 39
hell, 1, 30
hinders, 53
Holiness, 7, 8
holy, 7, 8, 15, 16, 32, 33, 40, 52, 87
Holy Spirit, 26, 31, 34, 38, 39, 40, 59, 62, 63, 64, 65, 67, 68
honest, 74
honor, 22, 87, 88, 89, 92
honoring, 87, 88, 89
human, 6, 8, 25, 64
humanity, 46
humility, 20, 52, 89
hungry, 23
hurt, 30, 85
husband, 17, 29, 99
hymns, 49
hypocrites, 13

I

identify, 2, 84
idolatry, 22
immature, 41
immortality, 22
impeached, 30
importance, 67, 72, 87, 92, 96, 98
impossible, 7, 41, 79, 82
improve, 59
impulses, 56, 57
indignation, 10, 22
inheritance, 2
iniquity, 16, 48, 62
innocence, 29

insecurity, 80
instructions, 37, 83, 84
insulted, 10
interest, 74
interpret, 60, 63, 64
Isaiah, 12, 26, 27, 50, 51
Israelites, 95

J

Jesus, 3, 4, 6, 7, 8, 9, 10, 13, 14, 16, 21, 26, 30, 31, 34, 38, 39, 41, 42, 43, 46, 48, 49, 50, 51, 53, 61, 62, 64, 65, 68, 72, 73, 75, 76, 77, 78, 79, 82, 83, 84, 85, 87, 88, 98
Job, 29, 30
Joseph, 60, 61
Joshua, 42, 53, 58, 65, 99
joy, 47, 48, 49
judgment, 1, 3, 10, 77

K

kindness, 47, 52, 54
Kingdom of God, 1, 98
knowledge, 9, 16, 17, 18, 59, 60, 61, 62, 63

L

laborers, 96
lamb, 51
lawlessness, 9, 13
laws, 23, 30, 65
Lazarus, 65
leader, 68, 98

learn, 6, 16, 20, 22, 29, 40, 41, 46, 47, 62, 89, 95
longsuffering, 47, 50, 51, 52, 53
Lord, 6, 8, 9, 10, 13, 15, 16, 17, 19, 20, 25, 26, 29, 30, 31, 32, 34, 35, 36, 38, 40, 41, 43, 48, 50, 51, 59, 60, 64, 68, 71, 75, 77, 78, 87, 88
love, 9, 15, 31, 47, 48, 49, 56, 60, 75, 84, 89
loyal, 54
lusts, 2, 7, 46, 47, 88

# M

marital problems, 61
Mark, 6, 14, 31, 37, 78, 81
married, 99
Master, 85
medicine, 64
meditate, 79
meekness, 52, 55
Melchizedek, 95
membership, 71, 72, 94
memberships, 71
mentor, 98
mentoring, 90
mercy, 10
Merriam-Webster dictionary, 4
Messiah, 43
mind, 2, 3, 7, 18, 20, 21, 27, 31, 34, 36, 40, 41, 46, 49, 55, 71, 75, 77, 84, 87, 89
ministers, 84
ministry, 65, 90, 92, 93, 94, 95, 98, 99
miracles, 60, 65
miraculous, 4, 5
module, 23, 24, 43, 45, 90, 94
monarch, 26

monetary, 90
money, 62, 88, 91, 92, 94
moral, 32
mouth, 6, 35, 51, 83
murmur, 51
mysteries, 40, 60, 63

N

nature, 2, 5, 6, 46, 65
new creation, 3, 4, 46
news, 4
noble, 79
nose, 72

O

obedient, 7, 68
offended, 79, 81, 82, 83, 84, 85
offender, 84, 85
offense, 50, 79, 80, 81, 82, 83, 84
offerings, 15, 71, 72, 78, 93, 94
offspring, 89
Omnipotent, 27
Omnipresent, 27
Omniscient, 27
opposition, 7, 20
organs, 72
overcome, 16, 47, 53, 84

P

pain, 29, 49, 85

Parable, 54, 85
paramount, 9
passage, 8, 15, 21, 22, 48, 54, 83, 90, 91, 93, 96
passions, 47
Pastor, 68, 81, 82
patience, 49, 50, 52
Paul Valentine, 99
peace, 22, 47, 49, 50, 79
Peace, 26, 49, 50
Persons, 26, 35
perverse, 51
Petition, 36
Pharaoh, 60, 61
pollute, 84
possessions, 29, 49
potentate, 26
power, 2, 3, 29, 34, 38, 64, 65
praises, 74
praiseworthy, 79
prayer, 5, 12, 13, 22, 23, 34, 35, 36, 37, 77
prayers, 19, 34, 35, 36, 37, 92
prays, 5, 40, 76
prediction, 62, 63
preferences, 74
presence, 6, 17, 19, 48
Presidents, 30
pride, 80, 89
priest, 95
Prince of Peace, 50
prison, 49
problem, 15, 68, 79, 82
profession, 13
prophecies, 63, 90

prophecy, 60, 61, 62, 63, 64, 68, 69, 90, 91, 92
prophesied, 13, 38, 61
prophet, 66
punishment, 1, 10, 86

## Q

quality, 5, 25
quarrel, 20
quote, 21

## R

ransom, 72
rebuke, 64, 68
Red Sea, 65
regeneration, 15
rejected, 10, 31, 33
rejection, 80
rejoice, 19, 48, 51
relationship, 25, 33, 34, 72
repent, 6, 10, 15, 20, 21, 36, 87
repentance, 6, 18, 19, 20, 21, 38
reprobate, 20
resolution, 84
respect, 87
responsibilities, 1, 72
responsibility, 48, 67, 75
revelation, 7, 29, 60, 61
righteousness, 16, 41, 46, 98
rods, 49
ruler, 26
rules, 18, 68

## S

sacrifice, 9, 10, 64
sadness, 19, 48
salvation, 1, 2, 3, 4, 5, 8, 10, 11, 12, 13, 14, 15, 16, 17, 18, 19, 22, 23, 26, 31, 38, 39, 43, 86, 89
Samaritan, 54
Samuel, 35, 66, 91, 92
Sapphira, 61
Satan, 2, 3, 26, 29
Saul, 64, 66
Savior, 16, 29, 30, 31, 34, 47
scream, 68
Scripture, 1, 2, 8, 10, 14, 16, 20, 21, 23, 26, 38, 41, 42, 49, 52, 54, 63, 64, 65, 66, 73, 77, 78, 85, 87, 88
seductress, 8
Seers, 65
self-control, 8, 47, 56, 57, 58, 59
self-discipline, 57
self-examination, 21
seminars, 90
servant, 20, 27, 54, 55, 74, 85, 86, 91, 92
serve, 29, 40, 72, 73, 74, 75, 78, 79, 88
sexual immorality, 87
shoulder, 26
sick, 82
Silas, 49, 81
Simon, 62
sin, 1, 3, 8, 9, 10, 11, 12, 14, 16, 17, 18, 19, 21, 28, 29, 32, 36, 46, 47, 84
sinful acts, 88
sinner, 14

sinners, 46
slaves, 16
sorrow, 19, 56
soul, 6, 14, 15, 17, 22, 26, 27, 31, 43, 50, 75, 80, 84, 87
sovereign, 26, 29, 31
sovereignty, 29, 31
spiritual gifts, 13, 59, 60, 61, 62, 67, 68, 74
Spiritual gifts, 60, 68
spiritually dead, 1, 2
stability, 76
standards, 18, 30, 44
statutes,, 4
steadfast, 54, 76
strength, 31, 56
stressful, 36
study, 6, 7, 20, 21, 28, 42, 78
suffering, 50
supernatural utterance, 62, 63
Supplication, 36

T

tax collector, 83
teach, 20, 35, 57, 58, 59
teacher, 98
teaching, 5, 9, 21, 68, 73, 90
teeth, 72
temper, 32
tempt, 19
Ten Commandments, 18
tender mercies, 52
tenderness, 56
theatrics, 68

thoughts, 29, 44, 57, 79, 80
tithes, 71, 72, 78
toenail, 74, 75
tongues, 38, 39, 40, 60, 63
transformed, 40
trembling, 23
trespasses, 1, 2, 3, 85
trials, 49
tribulation, 9, 22
tribulations, 53
troubled, 13, 49
trustworthy, 54
truth, 9, 14, 20, 21, 22, 48, 57, 98
two-edged sword, 43

U

unbelief, 64
uncleanness, 22
united, 77
unity, 77, 78, 83
unrighteousness, 22
unsaved, 2
usher, 92

V

victim, 81
vine, 7
violated, 86
vipers, 13
viruses, 79
visions, 65

vocabulary, 82
vow, 76

W

weaknesses, 34
wealth, 29
weary, 75
wisdom, 56, 59, 61, 62
witnesses, 10, 38, 83
wonders, 13
world, 1, 5, 8, 9, 16, 19, 25, 48, 49, 51, 53, 61, 76, 77
worship, 32, 36, 73, 81
worshipped, 25
wrath, 2, 3, 22

Y

yoke, 75